Hunting Wild Bees

Hunting Wild Bees

*How to track bees, harvest honey and
beeswax, and domesticate swarms*

ROBERT E. DONOVAN

WINCHESTER PRESS

To Kevin, who found our first bee tree. He thinks he's the best bee hunter in the Blue Ridge Mountains, but he's not. He's the second best.

Copyright © 1980 by Robert E. Donovan
All rights reserved

Library of Congress Cataloging in Publication Data

Donovan, Robert E
Hunting wild bees.

Includes index.
1. Bee hunting.   I.   Title.
SF537.D66   638'.1   80-15365

ISBN: 0-87691-310-9

Published by Winchester Press, Inc.
1421 South Sheridan
P.O. Box 1260
Tulsa, Okla. 74101

Printed in the United States of America

A Talisman/Winchester Book

Book design by The Etheredges

1 2 3 4 — 84 83 82 81 80

Contents

PHOTOGRAPHY CREDITS

Foreword

There are very few people in this world who really need to know how to hunt wild bees. I suppose commercial beekeepers need to know. If the commercial beekeeper's colonies become diseased, it is important that he locate and treat or destroy any nearby wild colonies to prevent reinfection of his apiary. And in some underdeveloped areas of the world, bee hunting provides the sweets that are an important part of the family's diet. But few people really need to hunt bees as part of their livelihood. So why bother?

Why? Because it's fun. Bee hunting is a vigorous outdoor sport that challenges the skill and ingenuity of the would-be hunter. It's a great excuse to get outside and do some hiking in the woods and mountains. Writing about bee hunting in 1956, John R. Lockard said, "In your excursions through the forests, you are unconsciously getting the benefit of the greatest source in the world of physical perfection—God's pure air. . . ." In our super-sophisticated world, those words sound embarrassingly ingenuous. But maybe we've gotten too sophisticated for our own good. I tend to agree with Mr. Lockard.

I've taught my kids how to hunt bees. It's not a skill kids need to know to get by in life. Similarly, most kids today don't need to know that corn should be planted when the oak leaves are as big as a mouse's ear. And they don't to know how to make maple syrup, or how to cut firewood, or how to tell a white oak from a black oak. But I think their lives are a little less rich if they don't know these things. As our civilization has advanced, we've lost touch with many of the rhythms and cycles of nature. Every now and then we need to reestablish contact with things natural. Bee hunting is a good way to reestablish that contact.

Bee hunting's lack of compelling social importance gives a certain lighthearted spirit to the sport. There's something downright whimsical about tracking honey bes across a field of clover on a warm sunny August day.

And best of all, if you're lucky, your successes in bee hunting will entice you to try beekeeping as a hobby. The honey that your bees will produce is one obvious benefit of keeping bees. But if you've never kept bees, you probably don't appreciate the greatest benefit of this hobby. Bees are absolutely fascinating to work with and to watch. I refuse to admit how many hours I've spent lying in the grass in front of one of my hives watching the bees busily coming and going and industriously storing pollen and honey. I probably should have felt guilty just lying there, basking in the sun, while they were doing all that work. But I didn't. Not one bit.

The truth of the matter is that I love to watch others work.

ROBERT E. DONOVAN
Lynchburg, Virginia

1. What's a Honey Bee?

This is a book about bee hunting. Bee hunting is an activity that is as old as primitive man and, at the same time, is as new as tomorrow. Very briefly stated, bee hunting is the art of attracting wild honey bees to a particular spot where they are allowed to feed, and then following them from that feeding spot back to their home, which is usually in a hollow tree. The objective of this exercise for primitive man was to find the tree so he could cut it down and remove the honey. These early bee hunters gave little thought to the plight of the colony of bees, and the colony was often destroyed in the process. However, methods have since been developed that enable today's bee hunter to achieve his objectives without killing the colony. In fact, some of today's techniques result in two bee colonies where originally there was one. When today's bee hunter locates his bee tree, he can use it as a source of free honey, a source of free beeswax, and even a source of free bees for his apiary if he is inclined to keep bees. On the other hand, the bee hunter may wish to leave the bee tree undisturbed once he finds it. In such a case, the hunter will be taking his satisfaction from having spent a pleasant day in the out-of-doors and from having met the challenge of finding the bee tree. After all, the real challenge

1

of this sport lies in finding the tree. Once the tree is found, the removal of the honey and the capture of the bees is simply a matter of mechanics. All of these topics, and many others, are discussed in this book. But before getting into a detailed discussion of honey bee hunting, we must address one basic question: "What's a honey bee?"

WHAT'S A HONEY BEE?

The world is full of bees; there are 20-25,000 distinct species worldwide. In the United States alone, there are three to four thousand species. But of all the species of bees that exist in the world, only four species are honey bees and, of the four, only one is of interest in North America. To understand what is and what is not a honey bee, it is necessary to understand a little bit about how scientists name and classify living things.

To eliminate the confusion that would exist if they used the common names of plants and animals, scientists long ago adopted the practice of naming all plants and animals with a Latin name that is used by all scientists worldwide. For example, in this scientific system of nomenclature, the angler's rainbow trout is referred to as *Salmo gairdneri*. In this system, the first name, *Salmo*, is the name of the genus to which the organism belongs, and the second name, *gairdneri*, is the species. Similarly all the honey bees in North America are referred to as *Apis mellifera*, meaning that they belong to the genus *Apis* and the species *mellifera*. A more complete description of the honey bee would be to say that it belongs to the phylum *Arthropoda*, the class *Insecta*, the order *Hymenoptera*, the family *Apidae*, the genus *Apis*, and the species *mellifera*. However, it is common practice to use just the genus and species name, and hence our honey bee would be called *Apis mellifera*, or *A. mellifera* for short.

Through common usage, the term "honey bee" has come to mean any member of the genus *Apis*. This is not to say that other bees do not produce honey. Many other bees, such as bumblebees, do produce honey. However, only members of the genus *Apis* produce honey in quantities and in a manner that is suitable for large-scale exploitation by man. Hence, the name honey bee has stuck with the genus *Apis*.

Worldwide, there are four predominant species of honey bees. They are: the western honey bee (*A. mellifera*), the little honey bee (*A. florea*), the giant honey bee (*A. dorsata*), and the eastern honey bee (*A. indicia*, also referred to occasionally as *A. cerana*). The little, giant, and eastern honey bees are all native to Asia. The little honey

The honey bee, *Apis mellifera*, collecting nectar from a dandelion.

bee and the giant honey bee are somewhat more primitive than the western honey bee. Both build combs in the open, neither is suitable for introduction into a hive, and neither is an important source of honey. And since they build their combs in the open, both are limited to the tropics.

The eastern honey bee, on the other hand, is an insect with a highly developed social order, and it has been kept for centuries in Asia as a source of honey and beeswax. The colonies of the eastern honey bee are weaker and less populous than those of the western honey bee, and so the eastern bee is gradually being replaced in Asia apiaries by imported western bees. The only honey bee of interest to Westerners is *Apis mellifera*, hence in the remainder of this book the term "western honey bee" will be shortened to "honey bee" and it will be understood to mean *A. mellifera*. But the biology lesson cannot end here, because members of the species *A. mellifera* are not all identical and the differences are important to bee hunters and beekeepers.

RACES OF HONEY BEES

The western honey bee is believed to have evolved somewhere in Asia Minor from whence it gradually spread westward into Europe. The

bee populations that developed in Europe were, in some cases, isolated from one another by mountain ranges and other geographic
features. Over a period of thousands of years, these isolated populations evolved along slightly different lines. The resultant bees were
all still honey bees, but they had slightly differing characteristics. In
the terminology of the biologist, they were all still members of the
species *Apis mellifera*, but they had now evolved into distinct subspecies. In scientific notation, the subspecies are indicated by a name
after the species name. For example, one of the new subspecies
(commonly called the Italian bee) was named *ligustica*. Therefore its
full Latin name would be *Apis mellifera ligustica* or *A. m. ligustica*
for short. Of all the subspecies or races of honey bees that exist, only
four are of interest to Western beekeepers and bee hunters today. The
races differ in appearance, productivity, and disposition. The latter
two features are of interest to beekeepers for obvious reasons. The
differences in appearance are important to the bee hunter since these
differences sometimes enable him to determine whether he is on the
trail of one or more than one colony of bees.

The four races of honey bees that are of interest to the bee
hunter are: the dark bee (*A. m. mellifera*), the Italian bee (*A. m.
ligustica*), the Carniolan bee (*A. m. carnica*), and the Caucasian bee
(*A. m. causica*).

The dark bee is originally from northern and western Europe.
It is a large bee, very dark in color, and has a nervous disposition.
Because this bee developed in western and northern Europe, it winters well, but honey production from this bee is not as good as from the
other races, and its future with beekeepers will probably be limited to
providing stock for crossbreeding.

The Italian bee, as you might have guessed, evolved on the
Italian peninsula. This bee is smaller than the dark bee, much lighter
in color, and has a very prominent yellow coloration on the abdomen.
As a consequence, these bees are often referred to as yellow or golden
bees. The Italian bees are among the most highly regarded of all the
races. They are gentle and calm on the comb, they show little tendency to swarm, they build large strong colonies, and they make a
fine light-colored beeswax. About the only drawback of this bee is that
if the honey flow is poor late in the summer, Italian colonies will not
winter well and they may have to be fed.

The carniolan bee is a native of the Baltic countries. It is
similar to the Italian bee except that the yellow coloration is somewhat less pronounced. This is the most gentle of all honey bee races
and it is a good choice for beginning beekeepers. The carniolan builds

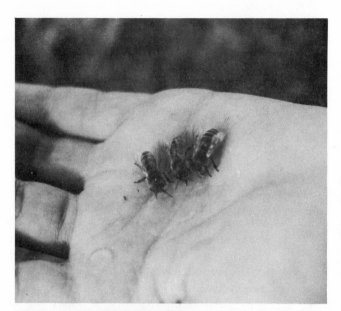

Honey bees are surprisingly gentle. They will readily take sugar water from the hand. The author often does minor inspections and limited manipulations of the hives with no protective equipment and without smoking the bees.

small colonies and it winters well since its food requirements are small. A disadvantage of the carniolan is that it has a strong tendency to swarm.

The fourth race that is of interest to the bee hunter is the caucasian bee. As the name would imply, this bee is from the Caucasus region of Russia. The caucasian bee is similar to the carniolan in appearance except that it is somewhat grayer. Like the carniolan, it is gentle and calm in the comb and it shows little disposition to swarm. There are, however, some disadvantages to caucasians. For one thing, they don't overwinter well. In addition, they have a tendency to rob other colonies and they make heavy use of propolis (bee glue) to cement the parts of their hives together. This is something of an inconvenience for beekeepers who desire to keep their hives in commercial hive boxes.

Although virtually all honey bee stock in this country was originally drawn from one of these races, the bee hunter is likely to find numerous crossbreeds in the wild. Bee breeders have carefully developed several hybrid strains over the years and these hybrids are specially selected to exhibit the best characteristics of the parent races. Some of these hybrids have swarmed from their commercial hives and are found in the wild. In addition, there is some crossbreeding among colonies of the various races once they get into the wild. Thus the bee hunter is confronted with every conceivable crossbreed of honey bee races.

Before leaving the subject of honey bee races, one other race should be mentioned. The bee hunter is unlikely to run across them in the woods, and they are not important commercially as honey producers in North America. But they have received more than their share of publicity lately. These are the so-called "killer bees."

"KILLER BEES"

In recent years, there has been a lot of publicity given to the killer bees that are said to be moving from South America, up through Central America, and allegedly are about to overrun the United States at any minute. We have seen headlines that proclaim, "Killer Bees Swarm Students." Newspapers and magazine articles have bombarded the American public with supposedly factual accounts of the ferocity of these demon insects. A 1976 UPI article said that the killer bee is "quick to anger and when disturbed swarms into enormous clouds and attacks any living creature within range." We have even been favored with *The Swarm*, a ridiculous and sensationalized movie about killer bees.

I expect that most people reading or seeing these accounts assume that the bees in question are some exotic or strange new species of bee—it just can't be the honey bee that is being described in these accounts! The bad news is that the so-called killer bees are a type of honey bee. The good news is that the accounts are so exaggerated as to be ludicrous.

In the previous section, four races (subspecies) of honey bees that are of economic interest to bee hunters and beekeepers were described: the dark, Italian, carniolan, and caucasian bees. There are, however, many other subspecies. One of these other subspecies is the African bee, *A. m. adansonii*, which inhabits the African continent south of the Sahara. As native honey bees have done everywhere, these bees have adapted themselves to their environment. The areas in Africa in which these bees live are often subject to drought. To escape the parching dryness of the droughts, the African bees regularly abandon their homes and swarm to be closer to seasonal sources of water. Since they swarm frequently, the bees are often forced to live for short times in the open while looking for a new home. As a result of this frequent exposure, the bees have developed a fairly aggressive pattern of behavior to protect themselves. To compound the bees' problem, they are heavily exploited by native bee hunters who steal their comb for the beeswax it contains. Central Africa is one of the leading suppliers of beeswax to the world market and most of that beeswax comes from wild colonies of *A. m. adansonii*.

In 1956, several African queen bees were brought to Brazil with the intent of producing a new hybrid line of bees. The idea was that the African bee, which was native to the tropics, when crossed with the European bee would produce a hybrid more suited to the Brazilian climate than were the European races.

The new hybrids did not prove to be a roaring success from a beekeeping point of view. They retained much of their propensity to swarm and much of their aggressiveness, both of which are undesirable characteristics from the beekeeper's point of view. And as you would expect with a strain of bees that was inclined to swarm, it was not long before several swarms had escaped into the wild.

The supposition of those who originally imported the African bee, that the hybrid would be more adapted to the tropics, turned out to be true. By 1973, the bee had spread to Venezuela, and by 1979 the bee was moving across Mexico heading for the United States. The bees that originally escaped were a hybrid of the African bee with various European races, and as the bee's territory has increased it has continued to crossbreed. Hence, the killer bees that we hear so much about are not really the African bee, *A. m. adansonii*. They are hybrids with some African bee in the lineage. For this reason and because they were introduced into Brazil, the bees are also sometimes called Brazilian bees or Africanized bees.

So who cares about all this anyway? Do these bees really pose a significant threat? The answer to the first question is that the people who seem to care the most about this spread of the Africanized bee are the people in the media who make a living writing stories. And the answer to the second question is that these bees pose little if any real threat to anybody. There is reason to believe that the northward march of these bees will be slowed or stopped as they move into colder climates since they are of tropical background and don't winter well. Even in those areas where they settle, they will be of little real concern. Most beekeepers raise their colonies from specially raised queens of controlled ancestry and they don't rely on the uncertain success that would result from the use of wild stock. As far as the bee hunter is concerned, the worst that can happen if Africanized bees settle in his area is that the bees with which he is dealing may be a little more ornery than if he were dealing with pure European stock. But some of the things that the bee hunter does, like cutting down bee trees and stealing honeycomb, get the bees so cross that it doesn't matter what kind of bee he's dealing with. That sort of activity is calculated to get any bee mad.

THE HONEY BEE IN AMERICA

The reader who has been following all this discussion about western honey bees has probably noticed that all of the western honey bees discussed so far are native to Europe, Asia, and Africa. What about the honey bees native to North America?

That question is very easily answered. There are no honey bees native to North America. All of the honey bees in the New World are the descendants of Old World stock. When the Europeans emigrated to settle the New World, they brought colonies of their honey bees with them. The first recorded introduction of honey bees into North America dates back to 1621; in Australia to 1822. The records of the Virginia Company of London dated December 12, 1621, reflect the following entry for a shipment of goods sent to their colony in the New World: ". . . we have by this shippe sent . . . fruit trees, as also pigeons, . . . and bee hives the increase thereof wee recommend to you."

Soon after the honey bee was introduced into a new area, some swarms would escape into the wild and establish themselves.

The bumblebee is probably the best known bee in North America because of its size and bright coloration.

Although it wasn't a native, the honey bee found the New World to be rich in forage and much to its liking. After their initial introduction into North America, the honey bees continued to spread westward, and Thomas Jefferson noted that the wild colonies managed to stay one or two hundred miles ahead of the western push of the settlements.

The fact that honey bees are not native to the New World has some interesting consequences. Since the bees are not native, no plant native to the New World is absolutely dependent on honey bees for pollination. This must be so since the plant obviously could never have evolved here in the first place if it needed honey bees. It is true, of course, that many of our native plants do better thanks to the honey bee, and it is also true that some of our imported plants do need honey bees. Another consequence is that in relocating to the New World the honey bee left many of its natural enemies behind. The honey bee did find a few new enemies, such as black bears and skunks, but by and large the bee came out ahead in the move.

OTHER BEES

In the United States there are seven families of bees which are further broken down into approximately one hundred genera and three to four thousand species. Most of these species are solitary in nature, but about ten percent exhibit some degree of social development. Many of these bees are important crop pollinators, although

The nest of the bumblebee is crude compared to that of the honey bee. This crudeness is one of the factors that has frustrated all efforts to produce useful amounts of honey from bumblebee colonies. Shown in the photo are: (A) honey pots, (B) pollen tube, (C) egg baskets, one of which is open, and (D) young brood in wax cells. The nest shown is of the species *Bombus morrisoni*.

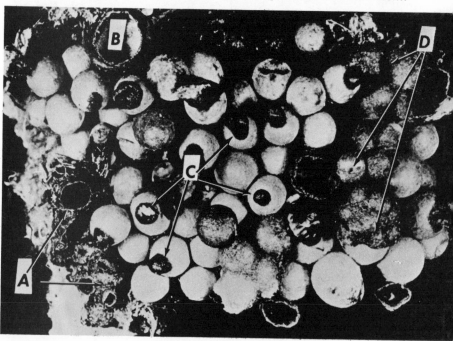

An alfalfa leaf cutting bee working on an alfalfa floret.
Note that the bee carries pollen on the lower part of her abdomen rather
than in pollen baskets on her hind legs as the honey bee does.

none of them are of great interest as honey producers. The bee hunter
will, however, in the course of his travels come across some of these
other species and a few are worthy of mention.

Of all our species of bees, the one that is best known to the
public is the bumblebee. This public notoriety is probably due to the
large size and distinct coloration of most bumblebees. Actually the
term bumblebee refers to any species of the genus *Bombus*, and there
are quite a few species of bumblebees, many of which differ sig-
nificantly in size and color.

Bumblebees form much smaller colonies than do honey bees.
A typical bumblebee colony will range from 100-1,000 bees, depending on the species. Even the biggest colonies do not normally have
more than 100 workers. Bumblebees are not as highly developed
socially as honey bees, and over the winter the entire colony dies off
except for one or more queens. These queens survive the winter by
hibernating, and the following spring they establish the new colonies. Bumblebee colonies are usually established in the ground. They
are occasionally a nuisance, and there are reported instances of
domestic animals being severely stung when they inadvertently

A female alkalai bee at the entrance to her nest.
The alkalai bee is an important pollinator of alfalfa.

stepped on the ground over a colony and a hoof broke through the ground into the nest area.

Bumblebees are very important and useful pollinators of certain plants. For example, the geometry of the red clover flower is such that the honey bee's tongue is not long enough to reach the flower's nectar. As a result, honey bees do not find red clover particularly attractive. But bumblebees find red clover to be an absolute delight. A healthy field of red clover can have as many as 200 million florets per acre and on a bright sunny day such a field literally hums with the sound of bumblebees.

Beekeepers and agricultural scientists have long been fascinated by the idea of establishing viable bumblebee colonies for honey production or crop pollination. But the small size of bumblebee colonies works against both of these objectives. In addition, the irregular shape of bumblebee comb would make large-scale honey extraction difficult.

Two other social bees of agricultural importance in the United States are the alfalfa leafcutting bee and the alkalai bee.

The alfalfa leafcutting bee was accidently introduced into the eastern part of the United States sometime during the 1930s. Within twenty years it had spread across the country and had reached California. This bee is small (one quarter to three eighths of an inch long) and is charcoal gray. Alfalfa leafcutting bees can be readily distinguished from honey bees by the fact that they carry pollen on the underside of their abdomens, rather than in pollen sacks on the hind legs as honey bees do. This bee is very useful in pollination of alfalfa, and in many parts of the United States alfalfa seed growers make special efforts to attract this bee and to develop colonies.

Alkalai bees are also important alfalfa pollinators, but they are not nearly so widespread as the alfalfa leafcutters. Alkalai bees are found in scattered areas mostly west of the Rocky Mountains and they are especially prevalent in large river valleys and poorly drained areas where alkaline soils are found. These bees are about the same size as honey bees, but are readily distinguished by the pale green bands across the back of their abdomens. As with the alfalfa leafcutting bee, extensive efforts have been made in some areas to encourage the nesting of this bee to aid in alfalfa pollination.

There are, of course, thousands of other species of bees. There are carpenter bees, "sweat bees," and mason bees. (I could barely resist the temptation to include spelling bees and quilting bees in the list.) But even a brief description of the major species is beyond the scope of this book. So we will now turn our attention to a detailed look at our quarry, the honey bee, and we will examine both its physical characteristics and its social order.

2. The Honey Bee Colony

The honey bee is one of the most interesting creatures on earth. Although man has exploited the honey bee since prehistoric times, little was known about the bee itself. This ignorance was due in part to the fact that the eastern and western honey bees establish their colonies and conduct most of their social activities in hollow trees and other dark places where they are difficult to observe. For thousands of years, many of the fundamental facts about the colony were unknown and mistaken beliefs were perpetuated. For example, Aristotle was mistaken about such a fundamental fact as the sex of the queen bee, and he wrote about her as the "king bee."

It has only been in the last two hundred years that we have gained a good insight into the life of the honey bee, and the real explosion of knowledge has come in the last fifty years. Some of this information is needed by the bee hunter if he is to be effective in his sport. Some of it is not needed by bee hunters; it is simply of interest to the outdoorsman and to the amateur naturalist because it will give them a better understanding of the world around them and the bee's role in it.

The honey bee colony responds and survives as a unit, and to

The three types of bees found in the honey bee colony are, from left to right, workers, queen, and drones. The bees are shown here in proper scale relative to one another. The workers are ⅜″ to ½″ long.

understand the functioning of that unit we must first learn about the three types of bees that make up the colony: queen, workers, and drones.

QUEENS

A typical honey bee colony is made up of one queen, about 100-1000 drones and anywhere from a few thousand to 70 or 80 thousand workers. The queen is longer than either the workers or the drones, although her body is not so big around and heavy set as that of the drone. As with the drone and the worker, the queen's body is divided into three segments: the head, the thorax, and the abdomen. Again as in the case of the drone and the worker, the queen has six legs and four wings, all of which are attached to the thorax. The wings of the drone and the worker extend nearly to the end of the abdomen, but the queen's wings extend only halfway back the abdomen. These differences in body and wing length are important to the bee hunter, since many of the bee capture methods to be described later are greatly facilitated if the bee hunter can determine the exact location of the queen. But don't let this description of the differences between the queen and the drones and workers fool you. When you are examining a piece of comb and there are thousands of bees scurrying over it and over the top of one another, location of the queen can be a real challenge. When commercial beekeepers raise their own queens or buy them from queen suppliers, they often have the queen marked with a spot of paint on the back of her thorax to make her easier to spot in subsequent examinations of the hive. Of course Mother Nature is not nearly so cooperative, and the bee hunter will be confronted in his labors with the task of locating an unmarked queen. Methods for doing this are discussed in later chapters.

The queen is the only perfect female in the colony. (I use the term "perfect" advisedly; a friend of mine contends there is no such thing.·You can bet that I don't touch that line.) The queen is the only female in the colony with a fully developed set of ovaries, and is normally the only bee in the colony that lays eggs. On rare occasions the workers (who are also female) lay eggs, but these eggs are always unfertilized.

When the queen in the colony becomes old and weak and her egg laying starts to taper off or she starts laying unfertilized eggs, the workers sense that something is wrong. They respond to this sense of uneasiness by constructing one or more queen cells in which they will raise a new queen. It is an interesting fact of bee life that any given fertilized egg can be raised by the workers to be either a queen or a worker. Whether the resultant bee grows up to be a queen or a worker depends solely on the diet that the workers feed the bee while it is developing. The eggs that are laid in the queen cells are fed by the workers in such a way as to insure that the resultant adult bee is a queen. After any honey bee egg hatches, it goes through two distinct phases, larva and pupa, before emerging as an adult bee. The larval stage lasts for about six days, and if the workers want the larva to develop into a queen they feed it a rich diet of "royal jelly" which is secreted by the workers. If the larva is to be a queen, this diet is fed the entire six days of its existence as a larva. If, on the other hand, the larva is to be a worker, it is fed royal jelly for only three or four days, after which it receives a coarser diet of pollen mixed with honey. This less nutritious feeding of the worker larvae results in the retardation of growth of their sex organs and stimulates the growth of pollen sacks on their legs, royal jelly glands in their heads, and other organs needed by workers but not needed by queens.

If the bees can raise any given female larva to be either a queen or a worker, the obvious question arises, "How do they know they have a female larva in the cell?" Or alternately, "What happens if there is a male larva in the queen cell? Do you get a 'king bee'?" The answer to that question involves one of the most interesting features of honey bee biology, parthenogenesis. Parthenogenesis is that distinctive characteristic of certain insects whereby both fertilized and unfertilized eggs will hatch and develop. In the case of the honey bee, the unfertilized eggs develop into drones (males) and the fertilized eggs develop into workers or queens (females). To make the situation

The peanut-like structure over which one worker is climbing is a queen cell. The wokers build queen cells in preparation for supercedure and for swarming.

even more incredible, the queen has the capability of laying either a fertilized egg or an unfertilized egg at will. She mates once in her life, before she begins laying eggs, and contains the sperm in her body the rest of her life. And in some manner that we don't completely understand, the queen is able to control internally within her own body which eggs are fertilized and which aren't. It is important that she be able to do so since drone, queen, and worker cells are all of different sizes to accommodate the fact that adult drones, queens, and workers are of different sizes. It would not do for the queen to lay fertilized eggs in cells meant for drones and vice versa.

Another aspect of queen rearing behavior that is of particular interest to bee hunters is the action that bees take if the queen is suddenly killed or is somehow lost unexpectedly. In such a case, there might not be any queen cells in development and none of the other bees in the colony can lay fertilized eggs. So what do the bees do?

They make emergency queen cells. This is done by finding larvae that are not more than two or three days old and expanding their cells to make them large enough to accommodate a queen. Remember that larvae that are only two or three days old have been fed a rich diet of royal jelly since they hatched from the egg. If this diet is continued through the larval state, the larva will eventually develop into a queen. By selecting several such young larvae, expanding their cells, and feeding them a diet of royal jelly, the colony can be assured of eventually having a new queen to replace the old one.

This emergency queen-rearing process is of interest to bee hunters because it is the key to success for one of the bee capturing methods described in a later chapter. In that process, the bee hunter captures the queen and as many of the workers as he can get and takes them home. The remaining workers are left in the wood with their brood comb. Realizing that they are now without a queen, the bees left in the wild will quickly select some young larvae and begin building queen cells. Eventually a queen will emerge from these cells that will insure survival of the colony. In this way the world winds up with two colonies where before there was only one: one colony that the bee hunter takes home and the one colony that is left in the world.

When the new queen emerges, one of the first things that she will do is destroy the other cells with developing queens. In addition to locating other queen cells by physically examining the combs, the new queen is aided in her search by a behavior known as piping. When piping, the queen emits a soft squeaky noise. Other queens that are still in their cells hear the queen piping and, whether out of combativeness or in response to some ingrained behavior pattern, they answer her piping. That response is their undoing. The newly emerged queen goes around to the unemerged queen cells, opens them, and stings the occupants to death. In some cases the queen is aided by the workers in the destruction of the extra queen cells. Unlike the workers, the queen can use her stinger repeatedly. She does not use it in defense of the hive; rather, she uses it almost exclusively to kill rival queens.

Occasionally, the new queen will immediately engage the old weaker queen (if there is one) in combat and kill her. In some instances, the new queen will tolerate the old queen for a short while and the colony will temporarily have two queens. Eventually the old queen will be killed or driven from the colony.

Sometime between three and five days after she emerges from her cell, the new virgin queen will take her nuptial flight. This flight usually lasts from ten to thirty minutes, and with the exception of a possible swarm later in life, the nuptial flight or flights are the only time the queen ever leaves the colony. On this nuptial flight the

In late summer or early fall, the workers chase the drones out of their colony where they will soon perish. This drone (foreground) was being chased out for the third time when this picture was taken.

queen will be fertilized in the air by one or more drones from her own colony or from other nearby colonies. After the flight, the queen returns to the colony and two or three days later she begins laying eggs. At the height of her egg laying activity, a healthy queen can lay as many as three thousand eggs per day.

The worker bees are attracted to, and to some extent are controlled by, the queen through several scents that she emits. These scents, called pheromones, control worker behavior in such ways as inhibiting queen cell construction, preventing ovary development in the workers, and stimulating the workers to feed the queen. These pheromones also serve as a sexual attractant to the drones. When a colony loses its queen and hence its source of pheromones, the workers are no longer inhibited from constructing queen cells, and they will start to do so in as little as four or five hours.

The average queen lives three to four years, although some have been known to live as long as eight years. However, older queens are usually poor egg layers and many commercial beekeepers replace the queens in their colonies every two years to insure that they have a vigorous egg layer in every colony.

DRONES

The drones are the males of the honey bee colony. They are heavier and bulkier than either the queen or the workers, but their bodies are not as long as the body of the queen. The drones have no stingers with which to defend themselves or the colony, no pollen basket in which to collect pollen, no wax glands from which to secrete wax for comb building, and a tongue that is too short for effective pollen gathering. Therefore, drones engage in none of these work activities. In fact, as best we can determine, drones do no work around the hive. They just sit around, eat honey, take occasional flights, and wait for a chance to fertilize a virgin queen.

But if you're thinking of applying for a job as a drone, don't rush into it. What you have just heard is the good news. Now comes the bad news. Drones have as their sole function in life the fertilization of virgin queens, but the one in a hundred that is successful in copulating with a queen pays for his moment of ecstasy with his life. In the act of copulation, the drone's sex organ is torn from his body (Oh, pain! Oh, suffering!) and he dies soon afterward. It is not uncommon for the queen to return from her nuptial flight with pieces of the male sex organ still protruding from her vagina.

And there is still more bad news. The workers in the hive realize that the drones are useful only as long as there might be a need to fertilize a queen. Therefore, they tolerate several hundred to a thousand drones in the colony during the spring and early summer when such a need might arise. But if the queen is healthy toward the end of summer and the workers begin to sense that no new queen will be raised, they begin to look askance upon the drones who now are viewed as an unnecessary drain upon food supplies. As the summer honey flow draws to a close and the nights start to get colder, the workers stop feeding the drones and they prevent the drones from getting to the colony's honey stores. At this time of year, it is common to see the workers pushing half-starved drones from the colony and the drones, thus expelled, soon die. The colony goes through the winter with few if any drones, and new ones are raised the following spring when a need might arise for their services.

The average life span of a drone, if he is not thrown out of the colony by the workers, is four to eight weeks.

WORKERS

Most of the bees in the colony are workers. A healthy colony will have 50 to 80 thousand workers, compared to fewer than a thousand drones and one queen. The workers are "imperfect" females in the sense that their sex organs are not fully developed, but they have other organs such as pollen baskets and wax glands that enable them to perform all the comb building, food gathering, brood rearing, and maintenance chores essential to the well-being of the colony.

The life cycle of the worker bee begins when the queen lays a fertilized egg in a worker-sized cell. After three days, the egg hatches and emerges as a white grub-like larva. The worker bees feed the larva with royal jelly and later with a mixture of honey and pollen as described earlier. About six days after the egg hatches, the larva is fully grown and it begins to spin a cocoon within its cell. At this time the worker bees put a beeswax cap over the end of the cell and the larva, which at this point becomes a pupa, goes through the next twelve days of its development in solitary confinement.

During the twelve days of pupal development, the body of the bee undergoes profound changes. Gradually the worm-like larva develops a distinct head, thorax, and abdomen and the legs, wings, and other external body features of the adult bee appear. Finally, twenty-one days after the queen laid the egg in the cell, the new

The worker bee develops into a fully grown larva (right) about nine days after the egg hatches and becomes a recognizable pupa with some eye pigmentation on the thirteenth or fourteenth day. The adult worker bee will emerge from the cell 21 days after the egg hatches.

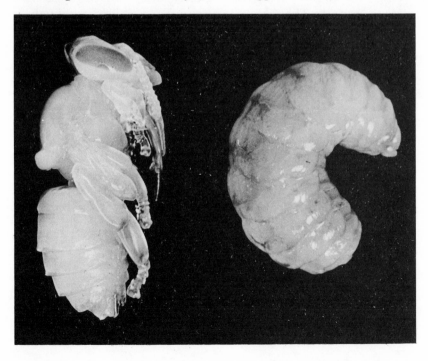

worker will begin to chew her way out of the cell in order to join the
working force of the colony.

Workers, queens, and drones all go through the stages just
described, but their schedules are somewhat different. The table
below shows how long it takes for the egg to hatch, when the cell is
capped, and when the adult emerges. Figures in the table are the
number of days after the egg is laid.

	WORKER	QUEEN	DRONE
Egg hatches	3	3	3
Cell capped	9	9	11
Adult emerges	21	16	24

Workers that emerge during the summer live from four to
five weeks; those born during the late summer and early fall will
overwinter with the colony and may live six months or more. The
short life span of the hard working summer bees is often attributed to
the fact that they "work themselves to death" or that they "burn
themselves out." Actually, it appears that the bees born during the
spring and summer are physiologically different from those born
later in the year. These physiological differences are brought about
by the differences in the brood-rearing activities and diet of the bees
after they emerge from the cell, and it is these physiological differences, and not the amount of work they do, which accounts for the
difference in life span.

ACTIVITIES IN THE COLONY

Honey bees have one of the most complex and interesting social
systems in the insect world. The tasks that the bees perform are
complicated, the order of the colony is impressive, and each bee is
dependent upon the activities of the others.

Certain bees in the colony perform specific tasks. This distri-
bution of work is sometimes referred to as "division of labor," but the
term is somewhat misleading. For one thing, it implies a degree of
central organization or control in the colony, and such is not the case.
The bees are not organized or controlled by any central group, or by
the queen, and they are not assigned tasks by anyone. Rather, each bee
is a separate automaton that is genetically programmed to behave the
way it does. It responds to the stimuli around it and within it
(heat, cold, hunger, hive odors, etc.) the way nature has programmed

A bee is born. This worker bee is emerging from the brood cell where she developed from egg, to larva, to pupa, to adult. She will immediately join the working force of the colony.

it to respond. There is no thought process such as engaged in by humans. Bees do not gather nectar and make honey so that they will survive through the next winter. They gather nectar and make honey because they are genetically programmed to gather nectar and to make honey; and they survive because they are so programmed. A bee does not know that winter is coming, and to say that it does is to romanticize and anthropomorphize the behavior of an insect.

Another reason why the term "division of labor" can be misleading is that the term can be misinterpreted to mean that one bee does one task or chore and continues to do that task throughout its lifetime. There is some "division of labor" among worker bees in the sense that certain bees tend, at any given time, to be doing certain tasks. But the segregation of work is done along the lines of age, and no individual worker continues to do the same chore throughout her lifetime.

In the first two or three days after it emerges from the cell, the new worker spends much of her time cleaning out empty cells. During this time she also begins feeding larvae. She continues to feed larvae

At times, the worker bees will be seen standing in front of the hive fanning it with their wings. The fanning causes air to circulate through the hive, cooling it and promoting thickening of the honey through evaporation.

until she is two to three weeks old. At that age her activities move away from nursing and more toward housekeeping. Bees in the housekeeping phase engage in cleaning debris from the hive, capping cells, standing guard, and packing pollen in cells. It is also during this phase that the workers begin to take their play flights. During play flights, as many as several hundred of these new workers will fly out of the hive and circle about it. They use these flights to fix the location of the hive once they begin their foraging flights. At the end of the third week, the workers become field bees and begin to gather nectar and pollen for the colony. The foraging period of the worker's life will last from one to three weeks, and she will continue to forage for the colony until she dies.

A field bee will collect nectar from plants by extending its proboscis into the nectary of the flower and sucking up the nectar. The bee will have to visit anywhere from 100 to 1000 flowers in order to collect a full load of nectar before returning to the hive. The bees locate the flowers using both their sight and their sense of smell. This latter fact is important to the bee hunter, for as we will see in a later chapter scents are very useful to the bee hunter when he is trying to bring the bees in to his bait.

The nectar that is collected by the field bees must undergo two changes before it becomes honey. The plant sugars in the nectar must be converted to a different chemical form, and the concentration of sugars must be increased by evaporation of some of the water in the nectar. The conversion of the plant sugar (sucrose) to simple sugars

Bees standing guard at the entrance to the colony will check incoming
bees to make sure they belong to the colony and to insure that
they are not robbers. Here a guard sniffs and touches a returning field
bee before allowing her to pass.

Honey bees will attempt to defend their colony against all would-be
robbers. Here some guards are attacking a bald-faced hornet.

(fructose and glucose) is accomplished by the bee through the addition of an enzyme called invertase. Some invertase is added to the nectar in the stomach of the field bee as she carries the nectar home and some is added by the house bees in subsequent manipulations of the nectar. The house bee receives the nectar from the field bee and places it in honey storage cells where it is allowed to ripen. During the ripening process, further conversion of the sugar takes place under the influence of the enzyme invertase, and the honey is thickened by evaporation of water. The bees speed the evaporation process by fanning the hive with their wings to increase air movement over the open cells of unripe honey. Once the cell is full of ripe honey, the house bees cap the cell with beeswax.

But what happens if the honey flow is strong, all the comb cells available for honey storage become filled, and the bees run out of storage room for their honey? Nature has an interesting way of taking care of this problem. If a worker bee is forced to retain excess honey in her stomach for too long a time, her digestive system will start to convert the honey into beeswax and the beeswax will be secreted through the wax glands in the bee's abdomen. The workers will then use this wax to build more comb for storage of honey. Thus, the wax secretion process is, to some extent, a self-regulating one. If the bees have enough room to store their honey, they will discharge it into the storage cells quickly and their bodies will produce little beeswax. On the other hand, if they are short of storage space and have to retain honey in their stomachs, their bodies will convert the honey to beeswax so they can build more comb. The production of beeswax is an expensive one for the economy of the colony since the bees must consume between six and fifteen pounds of honey to produce one pound of beeswax.

The beeswax comb that the bees build is another marvel of honey bee society. The bees construct the comb in vertical sheets that are about one inch thick. In the case of wild colonies, the comb is attached to the top or sides of the the tree cavity wherever the bees can find a secure surface. The bees build these combs in successive parallel sheets spaced about one and a half inches apart. This spacing leaves a "bee space" of approximately half an inch between the completed sheets for the passage of the bee.

The real marvel of the comb is in the details of the comb design. A sheet of comb can be thought of as a thin sheet of base beeswax with cells built up or "drawn" on both sides of it. Thus, the one-inch thick piece of comb mentioned earlier actually has openings of cells running down both sides. Each cell is a perfect six-sided

The western honey bee, *Apis mellifera*, almost always builds its comb in dark, protected areas. However, in some cases the comb is built and the colony sets up housekeeping wherever the swarm first lands. In cold climates, such a colony will not survive the winter.

structure and the cells are amazingly uniform. The hexagonal shape of the cells makes most efficient use of space while offering maximum strength. We don't exactly know how this interesting piece of honey bee engineering is done, other than to say that the ability to build the comb is an integral part of the bees' genetic makeup. In addition to making cell after cell in a perfectly uniform manner, the bees know how to build the cells in three sizes: queen, drone, and worker. There will only be a few, if any, queen cells in the colony, but there will be hundreds or thousands of drone and worker cells. In addition to raising brood in them the bees use the drone and worker cells for storage of honey. Pollen is almost always stored in drone cells. There are about twenty-seven worker cells per square inch and about eighteen drone cells per square inch.

Any social creatures must have ways of communicating with one another and bees are no exception. Since honey bee communication is quite complicated, a detailed discussion is beyond the scope of this book. There is, however, one aspect of honey bee communication that is of great interest to the bee hunter since, if it were not for this particular feature, the bee hunter would be out of business. This vital

aspect of bee communication is the ability of one bee to tell others in
the colony where she has found a source of food.

Foraging bees that return to the hive tell the workers in the
hive the location of new food sources by means of a "dance" performed
on the comb. The dance consists of a particular pattern that the bee
walks, combined with a series of body movements. If the food source is
close to the colony, the returning bee does a round dance which
consists of nothing more than running in a circular patter on the
comb. The other worker bees "observe" the dancing bee by feeling her
with their antennae and smelling her. The round dance greatly
excites the bees in the colony since the food source is near at hand,
and several will take off immediately in search of it. However, since
they know neither the direction nor the distance to the food, their
search is random; they know it's nearby.

If the food source is more than roughly 100 yards away, the
dancing pattern of the returning bee becomes more sophisticated in

In commercial hives, the bees can usually be induced to build
their comb in nice flat sheets. In the wild, they still tend to build in
flat sheets, but there are many more irregularities, tunnels,
and passages through the comb.

order to communicate information about the direction and distance to the food source. This more complicated dance pattern is referred to as the "wag tail dance" and it derives its name from the fact that during the dance the bee wiggles or "wags" her body back and forth. This dance is also run in a circular pattern, but every time she runs half way around the circle, the dancing bee cuts across the diameter of the circle. Then she runs the other half of the circle and again cuts across the diameter. The direction relative to the vertical of this run across the diameter of the circle tells the other bees the direction of the food source relative to the sun. For example, if the food source is in the direction of the sun, the straight run is done in the upward direction. If the food source is directly away from the sun, the straight run is done downward. And if the direction of the food source is at some angle relative to the sun, the straight run of the dance is done at the corresponding angle to the vertical.

The distance to the food source is communicated by the speed of the dance: the slower the dance, the greater the distance. The distance is also communicated by means of a series of noises that the dancing bee makes while she dances. The faster the noises, the closer the food. The dancing bee also gives her fellow workers other hints to help them find the new food source. She will give them samples of the nectar she has collected. This gives them an idea of the scent and taste of the food source for which they will be looking. By smelling the body of the dancing bee, the workers can get a further idea of the scent of the food source. Once they have obtained an idea of the scent of the source, the bees will tend to look for this smell to the exclusion of all others. This is important to bee hunters for, as will be seen in Chapter Four, scents play an important role in bee hunting.

The worker bees that stand guard at the entrance to the colony will try to defend the colony against all invaders, including bees from other colonies. But sometimes a colony becomes so weakened that it is unable to defend itself and then robber bees from other colonies will invade it and steal its stores of honey after killing the members of the weakened colony in the process. It usually takes the invading bees no more than one to four days to completely remove all the honey from the overrun colony. This propensity to engage in robbing is another characteristic of which the bee hunter can take advantage. As will be seen in Chapter 8, it provides a means of removing honey from colonies that have taken up residence in houses or in trees that cannot be damaged or destroyed.

Another feature of bee behavior that is useful to the bee hunter is water gathering. In the spring, before the nectar begins to

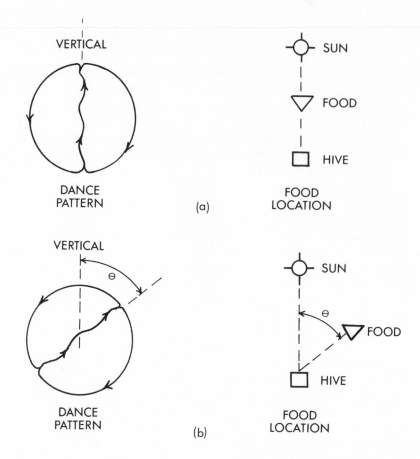

VERTICAL

DANCE
PATTERN

(a)

SUN

FOOD

HIVE

FOOD
LOCATION

VERTICAL

DANCE
PATTERN

(b)

SUN

θ

FOOD

HIVE

FOOD
LOCATION

Bees communicate to other workers the location of a source of
nectar by means of the wag-tail dance. The direction of the straight
run of the dance relative to the vertical tells the other bees the
direction of the nectar source relative to the sun.
The speed of the dance and the noises emitted by the dancer
communicate the approximate distance to the food source.

flow, the bees find that they need water to dilute the honey that is
being fed to the brood. Similarly, toward the end of summer, when
most of the honey flow is over, the bees may again find that they need
water, especially if the weather is hot, since the water is also used to
cool the colony by evaporation. When the colony needs water, workers are sent to the field to collect it just as they collect nectar at other
times. A large colony may have as many as 500 to 1000 bees out
collecting water and they can collect anywhere from one to two
pounds of water per day. The bee hunter uses this water collecting
behavior of bees to his advantage by locating his bees at water

sources during those times of year when the bees are not actively working on plants. Another advantage to the bee hunter of starting his hunt with bees that are taking on water is that the bees usually manage to find a water source quite close to home and thus the bee hunter does not have so long a tracking job ahead of him.

SWARMING

In preparation for swarming, the bees will raise one or more new queens. Before the first new queen actually emerges, the old queen, along with 40 to 90 percent of the workers, will fly off in search of a new home. Sometimes scout bees will locate a new home in advance and the bees will fly directly to it. More frequently, the swarm will fly only a short distance and then land on a branch, fence, or some other object. Here the swarm will form a large sack-like cluster and here it will stay until the scouts find an acceptable new home. Usually this takes no more than a few hours.

After the prime (first) swarm has left the original hive, one of the unemerged queens will eventually hatch to service the old colony. Now we have two colonies where originally we had one. The new queen will immediately begin to search for the cells of the other unemerged queens and destroy them. In some cases, she is aided in this task by the worker bees who are anxious to return the colony to a state of normalcy. In other cases, the workers will keep the new queen from destroying all the unemerged queen cells. When these other queens emerge, a second or even a third swarm may issue from the original colony. These after-swarms issue at roughly one-week intervals.

The bee hunter can use a swarm for either of two purposes. First, if he is inclined to keep bees, the swarm can be captured easily as explained in Chapter 8. Second, even if the bee hunter is just looking for bee trees and does not wish to keep bees, a swarm in an area where there are no apiaries is a sure sign that there is a bee tree near at hand.

A swarm of bees issuing from a tree is an impressive sight. The beginner might be somewhat intimidated by the number of bees and all the activity, but bees that are swarming are engorged on honey, quite gentle, and easily handled. Most experienced beekeepers do not even bother to wear protective clothing when working with swarms. Rather than being alarmed at the sight of a swarm, the outdoorsman and naturalist should view a swarm as one of those reassuring activities whereby Nature insures the survival of her

When bees swarm, they often do not go directly from the old colony to
the new one. In such cases the queen will land somewhere, such as on a branch,
and the other bees will cluster around her while scout bees are sent
out to look for the new home. This swarm, which landed in an apricot tree,
weighed 21 pounds and had over 60,000 bees in it.

species. Each year some wild bee colonies die. They are killed by bears, man, disease, cold winters, forest fires, and other disasters. Little by little all of the colonies would be killed off if Nature didn't provide a mechanism for increaisng the total number of colonies. Swarming is that mechanism.

THE SEASONAL LIFE CYCLE OF THE COLONY

Spring is a time of reawakening for the plants upon which the honey bee feeds, and it is likewise a time of reawakening of the honey bee colony. As the sun climbs in the sky and the bee tree gets warmer, the winter cluster of bees begins to spread out and some of the bees will begin to take exploratory flights in the warmest part of the day. These first flights begin when the air temperature gets up to about 50°F, which in the latitudes of Virginia means sometime between late February and the end of March. While they are in the winter cluster, the bees will not defecate and they use these early spring flights for this purpose. If there is still some snow upon the ground,

When bees begin to cluster on the front of a hive or bee tree in large numbers, it is an indication that something is wrong in the colony and it may be an indication that they are about to swarm.

the bee hunter is likely to find a circle of brown bee droppings in the snow around the bee tree, and he will also probably find some dead bees in the snow. These are old or weakened bees who embarked upon their first spring flight and were unable to get back, or bees who took flight on a cold day, unwisely decided to land, and then stiffened up from the cold and were unable to return home.

But the colony can tolerate these losses. The colony will soon have to tolerate much heavier losses, for as the spring wears on many of the worker bees that overwintered with the colony will die before the new brood can hatch. But the new brood will hatch, and as the spring honey flow begins, the strength of the colony will start to build. Beekeepers refer to this as the period of spring buildup. If the colony has a young healthy queen, by the beginning of the main honey flow the population will be up to or approaching full strength. Through selective feeding, medication, and manipulation of hives and queens, the beekeeper can insure that the bees in his apiary are at peak strength and efficiency when the main honey flow begins. Bees in the wild have the benefit of no such benevolent management, yet they manage to struggle by from year to year on their own. One sometimes suspects that bees knows a lot more about beekeeping than beekeepers do.

April is a time of anticipation for bee hunters where I live. The bees have made their first tentative flights, but no major honey flows are in progress. Yet the hints are there. Sometime between April 20th and 25th, the tulip poplar leaves will be about the size of a cat's paw, and the tulip poplar honey flow, which is the first major honey flow of the year, won't be far behind. About May 8th, the first tulip poplar flowers open, and then the bees start working in earnest. This is a great time of year for the bee hunter to begin his outings in search of bees. The bees are hungry and they are easily attracted by scents. And the woods are beautiful at this time of year. The redbuds are past their prime by early May, but the mountain laurel and the dogwood are in flower. The trees and plants are that shimmery brilliant shade of green that is found only in early spring, before the leaf miners get to the locusts and the heat and drought of summer get to everything. The bee hunter can make good use of this season by combining a pleasant stroll through the woods with his first attempts to make contact with the elusive wild bee.

As summer progresses, the bees will continue to build up colony strength and store honey. If their colony becomes overcrowded, or if their old queen becomes weak, the bees may be tempted to raise another queen and to swarm. This usually happens during the strong honey flows of May and June. Toward the end of summer, the honey flows tend to dry up in most areas, although in some locales there is a fairly strong fall flow. As the flow begins to dry up, the workers become less tolerant of the drones and start to evict them. If there is a fall honey flow in September and October, the bees will take advantage of it to get in their last stores before winter. The bee hunter can likewise be active as long as the bees are flying. This gives the bee hunter a season of at least six months over most of the country and considerably more than that in the southern latitudes.

Then comes the honey bees' toughest season: winter. In some parts of the honey bee's range, the temperature on cold winter nights gets down to $-20°F$ or lower and the icy winter wind fairly whips through the woods. The bees form a large ball or winter cluster on the combs in the center of the colony. The bees on the inside of the cluster eat honey and heat the cluster with their body heat. The bees on the outside of the cluster try to keep their head and thoraces inside the ball to keep warm. Periodically a bee in the center of the cluster will move to the outside and allow one of the outside bees into the cluster. Sometimes the outside bees get so numb they can't move, in which case the warm inner bees will pull them into the warmth of the cluster. If the colony's store of honey holds out, so it will continue in this fashion until spring. The inner bees will eat honey and the cluster will be kept warm by the heat they generate. But if the honey runs out, the colony runs out of fuel. When that happens, the flame of warmth in the center of the colony slowly goes out. Little by little the winter cluster gets colder and the bees on the outside of the cluster freeze to death. Eventually the entire colony, including the unborn brood, will freeze to death.

STINGS

Bees are unemotional. They don't get mad. They just do what they are programmed to do. And they are programmed to sting when they feel that the colony is in danger or their own lives are in danger.

Commercial and hobby beekeepers find that they can manipulate their colonies, often with little or no protective clothing, with no fear of being stung. Not so the bee hunter. The bee keepers are careful and slow in their movements and they avoid jarring the hives and upsetting the bees. The actions of the bee hunter who lays his ax and spitting wedge to the tree are guaranteed to activate the most docile of bees.

The sting apparatus of the worker bee is a modified oviduct

and therefore drones cannot sting. The stinger itself consists of two side-by-side pointed spears, each of which has barbs on the side. When the bee prepares to sting,she settles on the skin or clothing and starts getting a firm grip with her claws. Once this grip is secured, she begins to push in the stinger. As soon as one or more of the barbs on either half of the stinger grabs hold, the bee has what she wants. The two halves of the stinger can be moved independently. The foothold that is gained by one side of the stinger is used to push in the other half of the barb. Then that half of the barb is held still and the first half is advanced still deeper. In this way the stinger is "walked" into the flesh. At the appropriate time along the way, the bee contracts the muscles around her poison sac and some poison is injected into the wound down a channel that runs between the two halves of the stinger.

Once the bee hunter is stung, his problems have just begun for he is now a marked man. There is in the stinger an attack pheromone, the scent of which incites other bees to attack. In addition to the pheromone in the sting, there is another pheromone in a substance secreted from the mandibles of the bees. Thus, even bees that are unable to gain a foothold to sting can leave a chemical calling card that encourages others to attack. It is not at all uncommon to be working with bees for some time with no trouble and then to be stung several times in rapid succession. The cause of the such behavior on the part of the bees is the attack pheromone.

Some people are highly allergic to bee stings and even one sting can be fatal. If you have any doubts as to whether or not you are allergic, you should see a doctor since treatments are available that, in many cases, will greatly reduce or totally eliminate the allergic reaction. However, the average person has little to fear from honey bee stings. Generally, such stings result in minor soreness and pain at the time, with some itching and swelling that will subside in about one week.

The best treatment for bee stings is to avoid getting stung. Protective clothing and equipment are described in Chapter 3. In addition to protective clothing, the bee hunter or beekeeper who will be working around highly agitated bees should avoid dark clothing and clothing made of animal fibers such as wool and felt since such materials seem to incite the bees to attack. If two layers of moderate to heavy-weight clothing are worn, the material is inconsequential since the bees cannot penetrate through two heavy layers of clothing.

What do you do if stung? First, brush the bee off quickly before she gets any more stinger or venom into you than is necessary.

In many cases you will feel the bee land and begin sinking her claws in and can brush her off before she gets a chance to sting. If you do get stung, you should remove the stinger as quickly as possible. Do not attempt to grab the end of the stinger with your fingers and pull it out since the poison sac pulls out of the bee with the stinger and you will probably only succeed in injecting more poison into yourself if you squeeze the end of the stinger. The stinger and poison sac should be scraped off the wound using a sharp edge such as a knife blade. If no such instrument is available, use a fingernail, making a scraping motion. Some people like to dress bee stings with baking soda, witch hazel, aromatic spirits of ammonia, or any of several commercial preparations on the market. I find all of them pretty ineffective. Just grin and bear it.

ENEMIES OF THE HONEY BEE

The honey bee is not native to the New World, and when it left Europe it left many of its natural enemies behind. There were, however, a few new enemies lurking in the Americas. The most spectacular of these is the black bear. The black bear is omnivorous, and long before the honey bee arrived from Europe the bears had learned to tear apart rotted logs and trees in order to get at the grubs and colonies of ants that were occasionally found inside. But the reward that the bear gets from tearing into an ant colony is nothing compared to the rewards of a bee colony. If the bear can get into the bee tree he will eat comb, brood, honey, pollen, bees, and all. His heavy coat protects him from most bee stings and the few stings that he gets on the nose, mouth, and other unprotected areas are a minor inconvenience at most.

In some rural parts of the South, it has been reported that bee hunters routinely carry rifles with them on their trampings through the woods, indiscriminately and illegally killing any bears that they come across. They consider the bears to be competition in the search for bee trees. It makes no difference if the bears are adult or cubs, in season or out. Not only is this practice totally repugnant morally and legally, it is also totally unnecessary. The great majority of wild bee colonies are in live trees that are hollow, but otherwise quite stout. There is little that bears can do to such colonies. It is only in the rare cases where bees are found in rotted trees, or in trees with very large openings, that the bear has much chance of success.

Where bears do their greatest damage is in the apiary. Commercial hive boxes won't stand up to the assaults of a bear the way a hollow oak tree will. In fact, they won't stand up at all. When a bear gets loose in an apiary he can have a field day, and the results can be both devastating and spectacular. He will tip over hives, tear apart frames, eat combs and honey, and leave a trail of total destruction behind him. Commercial bee keepers confronted with this problem have tried many solutions. For example, spiked honey was left in one bee yard. The honey was deliberately contaminated with a chemical which would make the bear very sick and cause it to vomit. The conclusion drawn from that experiment was that bears must like to vomit, since they just kept coming back for more adulterated honey. The only effective solution found so far is a well-built electrified fence around the bee yard.

Other animals that are bee enemies are skunks and opossums. Both are insect eaters and both will scratch at the entrance to the colony and eat any bees that come out to investigate the disturbance. Both animals can be nuisances around the apiary but they are more easily controlled than bears. The extent of their depredation upon wild colonies is not well known, but it is certain that some damage is done. Commercial beekeepers have reported that an adult skunk can eat as many as 17,500 bees (one half pound) in one night. Combine that fact with the fact that a skunk family can have as many as twenty members (adults plus young), and the potential for damage to a commercial apiary becomes apparent.

Mice, particularly white-footed mice and deer mice, can be a real problem to bees. If the colony is strong, it will defend itself against an invading mouse to the extent of stinging the would-be invader to death in some cases. But if the colony is weak, or if part of the colony area is unoccupied because of cold weather, the mice can gain a foothold. They will eat the comb and they will gnaw out large openings in the comb to build their nests. Such an invasion can do extensive damage to comb and brood, and may on some occasions result in the demise of an already weak colony.

Some of the honey bee's worst enemies are other insects, and the worst of those are from its own order, *Hymneoptera*. Many kinds of ants are attracted to honey bee colonies where they eat the honey and occasionally pollen and beeswax. Unfortunately for the bees, the ants are just as persistent and industrious as the bees are. But if there are not too many openings into the colony and if the colony is in good health, the bees can usually defend themselves against ants.

Other members of *Hymenoptera* that prey on bees are wasps and hornets. The genus of most concern to beekeepers is *Vespula*, some members of which are commonly called wasps or hornets. Included in this genus are several kinds of yellowjackets and the bald-faced hornet. These insects prey on the honey bees themselves as a

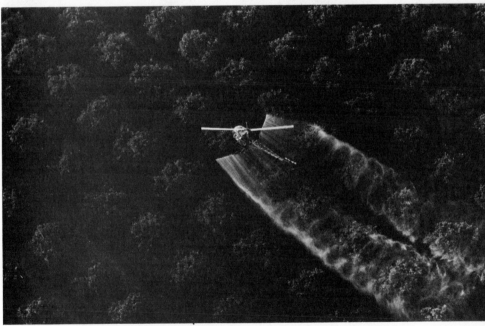

Although she left many of her natural enemies behind in Europe, the honey bee found some new ones in the New World. The most spectacular is the black bear, which can do incredible damage in an apiary and destroys wild colonies. Other enemies include skunks, wasps, and hornets. There are also five or six species of moths that can infest a colony and whose larvae eat the beeswax combs. Perhaps the greatest threat to the bee comes from pesticide dispersion such as this spraying operation in an orange grove near Lake Wales, Florida.

source of meat and on the combs as a source of honey. As with many other types of invaders, a strong colony can run them off. But a battle royal sometimes ensues, as evidenced by the fact that the ground in front of an attacked colony will sometimes be littered with the bodies of scores of wasps and bees killed in the struggle.

The honey bee and beekeepers in the Americas can be thankful that the mandarin hornet does not live on those continents. The mandarin hornet, *Vespula mandarina*, is indigenous to Japan and Southeast Asia. This hornet is about fifteen times as big as the honey bee and it preys on bees by waiting for them at the entrance to the colony. When a bee comes out, the hornet pounces on it and crushes it with its mandibles. It then flies off with the body only to return again shortly for another bee. If ten or more of these hornets gang up at the entrance to a colony, it is not long before the entire field force of the colony is wiped out.

Bumblebees can also be a problem. Instances are known of large-scale attacks on apiaries by bumblebees. In the cases cited, the honey bee hives had been staggered and opened up so as to provide additional air circulation in the hottest part of the summer. As a result of this opening up of the hive for ventilation, there were more openings than the honey bees could defend and the colonies were subjected to wholesale invasion by the bumblebees. Presumably similar unobserved encounters take place in the wild in situations where the honey bees are unable to defend their colonies.

In many ways, man is the honey bee's benefactor. In other ways, however, he is one of the honey bee's worst enemies. It has been estimated that the wild honey bee population reached its peak in North America during the Depression when many farmers abandoned their farms and pesticides were not widely used. As more and more land has been cleared and as pesticide use has become more widespread, the honey bee has had to struggle to hold his own. The woodland management techniques employed by some companies and individuals have also worked against the bees. These management techniques frequently call for cutting down all the old hollow "unproductive" trees in the woodlot, regardless of the need of bees, birds, squirrels, and other creatures which use them as den trees. Today, more enlightened methods call for selective retention of these trees, but such progressive methods have not as yet been universally employed.

The impact of pesticides on bee populations has by no means been limited to wild colonies. Domestic colonies, which are often closer to intensive agricultural activities, also suffer. For example, the pesticide poisoning situation got so bad that in 1970 in California approximately 89,000 colonies of bees were accidently killed by pesticides. As a result of this alarming trend, a state-wide educational effort was launched to make people more aware of the problem, and by 1974 the figure was down to 30,000 colonies. But even this figure represented six percent of all the honey bee colonies that California growers were using to fertilize their crops!

The 1970s was a decade of increased environmental awareness, and many efforts were made to reduce the adverse effects of the various chemicals and pesticides that were being dumped into the environment. But some of these well-intentioned efforts have worked to the honey bee's disadvantage. A case in point is methyl parathion. Methyl parathion is a deadly poison that is an effective pesticide, and it can be quite lethal to people as well. In 1974, the Environmental Protection Agency allowed a new form of this poison to be sold under the name Penncap-M. The new form was considered less dangerous to the people handling it since the particles of poison were encapsulated in microscopic plastic capsules. Once the pesticide was distributed in the fields, the plastic capsules would slowly disintegrate thereby releasing the enclosed poison to do its deadly work. But there was a problem with this scheme that no one appreciated at first. It turns out that the microencapsulated poison particles are just about the size of pollen grains. Therefore, they are picked up by bees in their nectar and pollen gathering rounds and they are brought back to the colony where they are stored as food. Normally, if a bee comes in contact with a poison in the field, she does not make it back to the colony. Thus even though that particular bee is lost, the colony is not affected. But the microencapsulated poisons make it all the way back home. And later the poisoned pollen is eaten by the bees and is fed to larvae, all of which die as a result. Some experts claim that there is enough poison in just a few of the microencapsulated poison grains to kill an entire colony. The effects of this poison are already being felt in areas where Penncap-M is used, and it is not clear just what the outcome will be. Various solutions to this problem have been suggested, but so far no final decisions have been made and Penncap-M remains as one more cloud on the honey bee's horizon.

Given all the enemies cited in this section one may wonder, will the little beast survive in the wild? In my mind the answer to that question is a resounding YES! The number of wild colonies will no doubt vary depending on land use, weather, imported pests, and other factors. But the honey bee is an amazingly adaptable and rugged little creature. His evolutionary history indicates that he was here on earth long before man. And if we are not careful, he'll be here long after we're gone.

3. Equipment

Winnie-the-Pooh didn't have very much success getting honey from the bee tree with his balloon. His problem was that he just didn't have the right gear. (His approach wasn't really all that great either.) This is not to say that a bee hunter needs a lot of specialized gear. He doesn't.

My son and I actually got started with articles that we either already had, or that we were able to make in our workshop. This chapter describes the equipment that is needed by the bee hunter, and places emphasis on making do with items that you already have or that you can inexpensively build. Bee hunting is meant to be a lot of fun, not a lot of expense. This chapter also describes in summary fashion standard commercially available beekeeping equipment. Such equipment is described here in just enough detail to insure that the novice bee hunter will understand such terms as supers, frames, and foundation when he encounters them later in the text. For a more detailed description of commercial beekeeping gear, the reader is referred to a book about beekeeping *per se*.

And rest assured of one thing. When it comes to robbing a bee tree, if you use the equipment described in this chapter and the methods described in subsequent chapters, you will fare much better than Winnie-the-Pooh.

PROTECTIVE CLOTHING

Honey bees are quite tolerant, but there are some things that they just won't tolerate. And some of those things that they won't tolerate are advocated in this book. So before you try them, it's recommended that you cover up.

The most important items of protective clothing are those that cover the hands and face. A long-sleeved shirt and long pants are generally adequate protection for the rest of the body. The pants should be tucked into boots, taped off, or sealed with elastic bands to keep the bees out. If you are particularly sensitive to stings, you may want to double up on pants and shirts. Recently I was working on a hive in my back yard and was in a rush so I didn't bother to smoke the bees first to calm them down. Part way through the operation I felt a sting in my back, right through a shirt and undershirt. A few minutes later, I got one in the leg right through my jeans. By the time I was done ten minutes later, I had collected seven stings—two through the shirts and five through the jeans. This was an unusual occurrence and my jeans were lightweight, but it does go to show that extra clothing is required to be completely safe.

To protect the face, some sort of headnet or mask is required. Even though beekeeper's veils are available commercially, I often use no more than a camouflage face mask, such as turkey hunters use. A hat should be worn under the mask and care must be taken it insure that the mask does not come in contact anywhere with the face. Bees have an uncanny way of finding such places and of stinging right through the headnet. The bottom of the mask can be tucked into the shirt or jacket.

The commercially available bee veils afford better vision and somewhat better protection that the impromptu camouflage mask or mosquito net mask. The commercial version is usually made in part of stiff screen, or has an integral frame to keep it from coming in contact with the face. One advantage of the camouflage net, however, is that it is less bulky and can be rolled up and stuck in the pocket.

Gloves must be long enough to overlap the cuffs of your shirt. There are many styles of hunting gloves and skiers gloves and mittens that will suffice. Get a pair that is washable or that has a surface that is easily wiped clean, since the gloves will get covered with honey soon or later. As was the case with the face mask, commercial

The hinged door on a transport box should have no holes in it. The far end, which is not hinged, should be screened. The screen will let air into the box, and in certain operations it will serve as a source of light toward which the bees will move.

beekeeper's gloves are available. They are generally rubberized or washable, come up to the elbow, and seal at the top with elastic. The serious bee hunter or beekeeper will want a set of these commercial gloves, but the part-timer or beginner can get by with gloves that he already has.

TRANSPORT BOX AND BRUSH

If the bee hunter plans to keep the bees that he finds, there are several ways in which he can transport them home. Depending on the technique that he uses to capture the bees and to remove the honey from the tree, he may find that the bees wind up on short pieces of log ("bee gums") or that they wind up in commercial hives for transportation home. However, some of the capture techniques described in Chapters 7 and 8 require that a box or container of some type be taken to the tree to carry the bees home in.

The bee transport box should be approximately eight inches square by eighteen inches long. These dimensions are not critical. One end of the box is covered with fly screen and the other end has a hinged door on it. The hinged door should have redundant latches on it to keep it closed, since one does not want a transport box full of bees bouncing open in the car on the way home.

Eyebolts should be attached to opposite sides of the box at both ends. These eyebolts can be used to attach the box to a tree when driving the bees from a tree into the box, and a rope chain can be strung through the eyebolts to serve as a handle. The outside of the box may be varnished or painted, but do not paint the inside since the bees will accept the box much more readily if the interior box has the smell of unfinished wood.

SMOKERS

The bees will be much easier to work with if you smoke them first. Beekeepers use smokers that are commercially available and which, if properly used, will maintain a fire for a long time. Such smokers provide a controlled and convenient source of smoke.

The beginning bee hunter can make a smoker for himself that will work quite satisfactorily. Start with a tin can that is three to four inches in diameter and is eight to ten inches long. You will also need some rubber hose between one half inch and one inch in outside diameter. About one inch above the bottom of the can on one side, cut a hole just large enough so that the hose can be forced snugly into the hole. In the other side of the can, about three inches higher, cut a similar hole.

To operate the smoker, fill it about one half full with leaves, wood chips, oily burlap or rags, or similar material and ignite it. To encourage the fire, blow into the lower piece of hose. You will need to wear gloves or handle the smoker by the pieces of hose (or add a handle), since the can will soon get too hot to handle. Once you have a fire started, place a lid or piece of wood over the can. If you now puff into the lower hose, you will find that you get a fairly decent, easily directed stream of smoke out the upper hose.

BAIT BOXES

The single most important weapon in the bee hunter's arsenal is his bait box. Traditionally these bait boxes have been flat cigar box-like devices. However, I have developed a vertical design shaped more like a milk carton and I find a box of this design much easier to use, especially when the bees are working on low-lying plants such as white clover and dandelion. Both designs are described here and you can take your pick.

The vertical bait box is about four inches by four inches by ten inches high. The bottom of the box is open and opens upon the lower

The side has been removed from this vertical bait box to show the path taken by the bee. The box is set down over the bee, trapping it in the lower chamber. The bee sees the light coming through the slit being pointed out in the picture. The bee then moves toward the light and into the upper chamber.

chamber of the box which is about seven inches high. The upper chamber of the box is about three inches high and it connects with the lower chamber by means of a narrow slit about 3/8" wide in the back of the box. The bottom chamber is completely enclosed except for its open bottom and the slit connecting to the upper chamber. The upper chamber has a one-inch hole in the top of it and the front of the top chamber is open.

In addition to the box itself, several additional items are needed. First, pieces of glass or clear plastic must be cut of such size as to cover the one-inch top opening and the opening in the front of the top chamber. Then pieces of wood (or other opaque material) must be cut to the same dimensions. When the box is in use, it will be necessary at various times to cover the top and front openings with either the transparent or opaque covers. Elaborate hinge and door type systems can be envisioned to allow the appropriate pieces to be put in place, but I find it much easier and quite satisfactory to just stretch and elastic band around the box and to hold the covers in place under the elastics.

You will also need a piece of bee comb cut to approximately three inches by four inches, such that it will fit into the top compartment without covering the slit in the back of the compartment. The best comb for such use is the durable black comb out of a bee tree. If you don't have any such comb on hand, you can probably get a piece from a beekeeper. Failing in this, a shallow container such as a jar cap will serve in a pinch.

Several final touches on the outside of the box will finish the job. First, a handle of rope or leather thong should be added to the box to simplify carrying and hanging it. Second, a coat of white paint (outside only) will make it easier for the bees to spot and return to the box. Finally, a few drops of anise oil scent, or of some other scent attractive to bees, sprinkled on the outside of the box will make it still easier for the bees to locate the box. The preparation of these scents is described in Chapter 4. How the bait box, its comb, and its covers are used to lead you to the bee tree is described in Chapter 5.

The other type of bait box is the flat or cigar box style. This box is basically a three-inch wide by six-inch long box that is three inches deep. A divider in the middle of the box divides it into two compartments, each roughly three inches by three inches by three inches. One compartment has a fixed wooden cover over it and there is also a one inch window in that end of the box. The other compartment has a transparent lid that is either hinged or can be removed as a separate piece. As with the vertical box, this box can be made of any 1/4" to 3/8" wooden stock, including plywood. As with the vertical box, it is important that pieces fit snugly and that they are light tight, since the principles of operation of the box depend upon being able to darken either compartment at will.

The front and rear compartments of the box are connected by a one-inch hole, and the box must be fabricated in such a way that this hole can be opened or closed from outside the box when the box is sealed shut. There are many ways that this can be done, but remember that whatever mechanism is used to cover and uncover the hole between the compartments, it must be designed to be operated with the box sealed shut and the mechanism must be light tight. One way to do this is to make a small wooden cover just big enough to cover the hole between the compartments. Attach the cover to a piece of coathanger long enough to extend out both sides of the box. Drill one hole in either side of the box just large enough for the wire to pass through without binding. These holes should be so positioned so that when the piece of wire with the wooden cover attached is slid into the holes, the cover will cover and uncover the opening between the two compartments as the wire is slid back and forth. If additional light sealing is needed, cut two one-inch square pieces of rubber out of an old inner tube and pierce holes in the center of the rubber pieces. Slide these rubber pieces over the ends of the wire and staple the rubber to the sides of the box. The wire will slide snugly through the holes in the rubber, thereby effectively sealing out all light.

The transparent piece (glass or plastic) covering the small

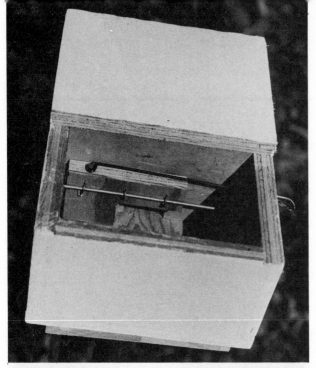

This is an old fashioned horizontal, or cigar-box style, bait box. The transparent front cover has been removed to show more clearly the slide between the compartments.

A broom handle, sharpened at one end and with a platform nailed to the other end, makes a handy stand for the horizontal bait box.

opening in the rear compartment can be fixed in place since there will
never be any need to remove it. It will, however, be necessary to cover
or darken this window. This can be done by stapling a rubber band or
a piece of wire over the window in such a way that an opaque cover,
such as a piece of wood or cardboard, can be slipped under it to cover
the window.

It will also be necessary to darken the front compartment that
has the large moveable transparent cover. This can be done by cutting a piece of wood large enough to cover the window in the front
compartment and then resting it over the window when the time
comes to darken the front compartments.

When the box is completed, the outside should be painted
white. Once the paint is dried, a little anise oil scent should be rubbed
on the outside of the box. When in the woods, it is often difficult to find
a satisfactory place to rest the box where it will be easy to observe the
bees working the bait. Therefore, a lightweight stand is a great
convenience. To make a stand, cut a piece of broom handle three to
four feet long and sharpen one end of it. To the other end, nail a six-
inch by six-inch piece of wood. This stand can be pushed into the
ground almost anywhere, and the bait box can then be rested on the
platform.

You will also need a piece of beeswax comb large enough to fill
or nearly fill the front compartment. The comments given previously
with respect to the piece of comb for the vertical bait box also apply
here.

HONEY SCENTING DEVICES

The employment of most scents requires no more than that they be
sprinkled on some leafy branches or a piece of cloth and waved in the
air. These methods, which are described in more detail in the next
chapter, will put enough scent in the air to bring in any bees that
happen to be in the area. But simply waving an object coated with
honey in the air would not put out much scent. Honey must be heated
to be an effective scent.

When honey is boiled slowly, it fills the air with a heavy sweet
aroma that bees find absolutely irresistible. The challenge that
confronts the bee hunter is to develop an uncomplicated lightweight
device that can be easily carried into the woods to heat the honey.
There are probably as many ways to do this as there are bee hunters,
and you will no doubt develop methods of your own. I offer three
suggestions as points of departure for your own experimentation.

A scent can is a simple device for heating honey and getting the honey aroma into the air. Note the bottle cap containing honey on the wire above the flame, and note the bee feeding on the diluted honey on top of the can.

Candles and fires tend either to blow out or to be hard to start. They also present a danger of spreading. I have found that far and away the most convenient heat source for heating honey is one of the self-contained propane or butane backpacker's stoves. The backpacker versions of this appliance are usually small, highly portable lightweight devices that screw directly on to the top of the can of fuel. If a stove is used, any small container, such as a metal jar lid, will suffice to hold the honey. Note that one does not have to heat large quantities of honey to attract the bees; a teaspoonful is quite adequate. If you don't have a stove but do have a lantern, you can still use it to heat the honey. You just have to be a little more imaginative. Such lamps will have one or more places on them that get quite hot. I have used the simple expedient of just dripping honey on the hot parts of the lamp. But this gets a little messy. It is much more effective to contrive some way to secure a jar lid or other small container onto the lamp in such a way that the honey can be heated in the container, leaving the balance of the lamp clean. Both the stove and the lamp offer great convenience in that they are easily lit and the heat level is adjustable. The honey scent works best when the honey is kept at a very low simmer.

If you don't have one of these backpacker's devices at your disposal and don't care to buy one, a less expensive expedient is the scent can. A scent can may be made from any large tin can. If the top

A little honey dribbled into the pool of molten wax at the base of a candle flame is another way to get the honey aroma into the air. This method works even better if the candle is made of beeswax.

of the can has not been removed, do so. Next a rectangular hole about three inches wide by four inches high is cut in the side of the can near the bottom. A candle will be set in the bottom of the can to heat the honey, but first a device must be installed in the can to hold the honey over the flame. An easy way to do this is to cut a piece of heavy wire or coat hanger to a length slightly longer than the diameter of the can. Then weld or braze the piece of wire across the open end of a jar lid in such a way that the lid is centered on the wire. Punch a series of evenly spaced holes up one side of the can and then punch a series of matching holes up the other side of the can. Then, from inside the can, insert one end of the piece of wire in one of the holes and the other end in the corresponding hole on the other side of the can. The height of the lid full of honey can be adjusted by placing the wire in a higher or lower pair of holes, and the heat being applied to the honey can be adjusted by sliding the wire back and forth so that the lid is more or less centered over the flame. I have found it useful to add a wire handle to the can for ease of carrying.

The third and simplest device for scenting bees is nothing more than a large candle three or more inches in diameter. Once the cancle has been burning for a while it will form a depression of melted wax around the wick. If some honey is poured into this depression, the air will quickly be scented with the perfume of warm honey. This method works even better if the candle is made of beeswax (see

Chapter 10 for instructions on making beeswax candles). Homemade beeswax candles often give off a honey-tinged scent even when no honey is added, and I have at times been successful bringing in bees just by lighting such a candle. However, it does work a lot better if you add some honey to the base of the flame. With any kind of candle, you should add as much honey as possible to the flame without extinguishing it.

BEE GUMS

Bee gums are short sections of hollow logs that are used to house bees. In the old days, it was common for beekeepers to keep their bees in

Old-time beekeepers used to keep their bees in hollow pieces of logs (gums) with minor improvements such as removable covers. This method is still used in some rural areas and, if legal in your area, it can be an interesting way to keep a colony of bees. Note, however, that honey production will not be nearly as good as in a commercial hive.

such devices since they usually found the bees in hollow trees to begin with. The trees were then chopped down, cut into short lengths, and brought home. In such a situation, the simplest and least expensive way to keep the bees is right in the log where they were found. Although bees can be kept in this way, the modern beekeeping equipment described later in this chapter produces colonies that are much easier to manage and that produce higher honey yields. Modern hives are also easier to inspect for disease and the bees in them are easier to treat if disease is found. For this reason, bee gums are not allowed in some states. But if they are allowed where you live, one or two bee gums will add a fascinating touch to your backyard, and the bees in those gums will be living essentially as they do in the wild.

This view down the inside of a bee gum shows the crossed sticks to which the bees will attach their comb.

The section of hollow tree will need some improvement if it is to be a first class home for your bees. The simplest thing to do is to set out two cinder blocks, place a board across the blocks, stand the log on the boards on end, and then place another board over the top of the log to keep the rain out. Sometimes, as when you have nowhere else to place the bees and the comb that are in the log, this is about all that you can do. However, the improvements that really should be made to the gum can only be made if the bees are first removed from the log.

The best bee gums are made from sections of hollow log that are two to three feet long and fifteen to twenty inches in diameter.

Assuming that you have an empty section of hollow log, begin by inspecting the interior of the log. Using a chisel (long handled if you have one), split out all loose and rotten material in the log. If the log is basically sound, chip out as much of the interior as you can and try to get the walls of the gum to where they are only two or three inches thick. This will give your bees maximum living space.

About halfway up the gum, drill four holes about one inch in diameter at 90° intervals around the gum. Cut some branches or saplings of similar diameter and insert them through the holes so that they form an X pattern when viewed from the end of the gum. Trim these cross pieces off so that they extend out of the gum two or three inches on each side. Once housed in the gum, the bees will use these crossed sticks as supports for their comb. They will raise brood in the area below the crossed sticks and they will store honey in the area above.

Some sort of cover must now be provided. To do so, nail a board about six inches by eighteen inches to one side of the gum in such a way that about one half of its length extends above the top of the gum. Then nail another such board to the other side of the gum directly opposite the first. Drill a hole about one inch in diameter in the center of each of these side boards. The hole should be about an inch and a half above the top of the gum.

Next cut a piece of board long enough to cover the top of the gum. If this board is not wide enough to cover the top hole, lay two boards side by side. This board (or boards) constitutes the inner cover, and the bees will attach their comb to it. This inner cover is held in place by a stick that is inserted through the holes in the side boards.

Next an outer cover or rain cover is needed. The rain cover is simply a wooden square made from several pieces of board nailed together with two strips of wood. The rain cover should extend three to six inches beyond the gum on all sides. The rain cover is placed on top of the gum and is propped up on one side to provide a slanted surface for runoff of rainwater.

Lifting the rain cover on the bee gum exposes the inner cover and the cross-stick that holds the inner cover in place.

If your gum does not have adequate branch holes or other openings for the bees, some holes should be drilled around the base of the gum. Eight or ten one-inch holes clustered toward one side of the log will suffice.

Finally, the gum must be set up off the ground to keep out termites and other pests. Elevate the gum on cinder blocks, railroad ties, piece of log, or other materials and place a board under the gum to close up the bottom hole. Once this is done, the gum is ready for the introduction of bees.

Rather than make these modifications to the top of the bee gum, some people prefer to combine the old with the new by attaching a modern commercial hive to the top of the bee gum. To do this, first

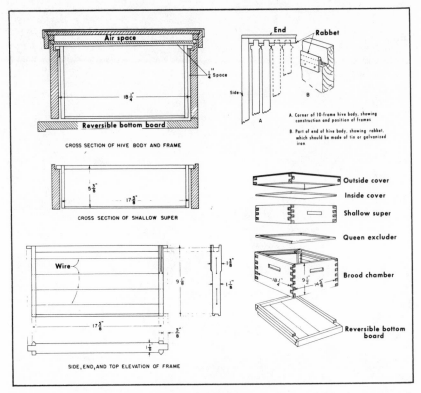

Commercial bee ware is fairly standardized and is available from several manufacturers. This figure shows the interrelation among the various pieces of equipment such as bases, supers, brood chambers, and covers.

insure that the top of your hollow log is cut off square. Then nail a 17″ × 21″ piece of exterior plywood, with a hole in the center of it, to the top of the gum. The center hole should be the same size as the hole in the center of the log. A commercial super is then rested on top of this platform. The bees will use the gum as a brood chamber and will store honey in the super.

MISCELLANEOUS

If the bee hunter plans to cut the tree down to get the honey and bees out, he will, as a minimum, require an ax. However, the job will go much more quickly if he takes along a chainsaw, and in certain cutting operations a couple of log splitting wedges can also be very helpful.

If the honey is to be taken from the tree in the woods, several buckets will be needed. Lightweight plastic buckets can be stacked one inside the others and are less of a burden to carry in and out of the woods than are the metal variety. How much bucket capacity you will need depends on how lucky you are in finding a tree with a lot of honey in it. Bee trees can contain anywhere from no honey to (rarely) fifteen or twenty gallons. Also take along a large metal spoon since the honey combs are frequently broken up when the tree falls. The spoon comes in handy for spooning out the mess of comb and honey.

It is handy to have a brush with which to brush the bees from the slabs of honey comb. Bee supply houses sell special brushes for this purpose, but any wide soft brush will do. I have a brush that is about ten inches wide that I use to clean my workbench, and it does a pretty decent job on bees.

BEE WARE

The bases, covers, hive bodies, and other equipment that is sold commercially and is used to set up beehives is collectively referred to as bee ware.

A basic beehive consists of a base board (about 16½″ × 22″) and a cover that fits over the hive. The hive body is a wooden box with no top or bottom, within which the beekeeper hangs eight to ten moveable frames. Each frame is about 17¾″ × 9¼″ and contains a slab of foundation material inside the wooden frame. The foundation material is provided as starter upon which the bees will build their comb. Modern foundations consist of a thin sheet of plastic which is coated on both sides with beeswax. The beeswax is impressed with a hexagonal pattern similar to that used by the bees in building their comb. The combination of real beeswax and a familiar pattern is sufficient inducement to get the bees to make most of their comb where the beekeeper wants them to make it.

The hive bodies come in several sizes. Most are approximately 16½″ × 20″ around the sides as described above, but they come in different depths. The two most common depths are 9¾″ and approximately 6″. The hive body in which the bees are raising brood is always one of the deep ones, and some beekeepers provide two deep bodies for this purpose. On top of the brood chamber or chambers, the beekeeper stacks one or more hive bodies in which the bees will store excess honey. These hive bodies on top of the brood chamber can be either the deep or shallow bodies, and they are referred to by beekeepers as supers or extracting supers. It is from these extracting supers that the beekeeper will harvest his honey crop.

Most beekeepers use an item called an inner cover between

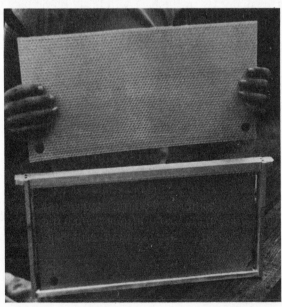

The foundation (above) is a thin sheet of beeswax or beeswax over plastic that serves as the base on which the bees build comb in a commercial hive. The sheets of foundation are placed in wooden frames (below) which are suspended in the hive body or super.

The components of commercial hives come in kit form and are easily assembled by a youngster.

A simple, bolt-together, adjustable frame of 2 × 4s makes a sturdy stand for a hive that is being furnished for bees trapped out of a tree. The hive is on hinged boards that can be adjusted in order to level the hive.

the uppermost hive body or super and the outer cover. The inner cover consists of a thin piece of plywood or masonite, with a frame around it that is sized so that the inner cover has the same outside dimensions as the hive body. The inner cover has an opening in the center that is about one inch by three inches. During certain bee handling and manipulation operations, the beekeeper places a device known as a bee escape in this hole.

A bee escape is a clever little device that allows the bees to pass through it in one direction, but not in the other. If it is placed in the inner cover, it allows the bees to pass from the upper hive into the lower one (if that's how the escape is oriented when it's installed), but not the other way. This is of interest to the bee hunter, because in certain bee capture situations, he will want to let the bees out of their colony in a hollow tree or between the walls of a building, but not let them back in.

Another commercial item of interest to the bee hunter is the bee feeder. The bee feeder consists of a hollow base that is open on one side and which holds an inverted pint or quart glass jar upside down above it. The jar lid has numerous small holes in it. The beekeeper fills the jar with sugar water, sets it upside down in the base, and the bees enter the base through the open side and suck the sugar water out of the jar through the pin holes in the lid. It is a good idea to feed the bees once they have been caught. The bee hunter can either buy one of these inexpensive feeders, or he can make one by punching eight to ten small holes in a jar lid, filling the jar with sugar water, and then turning the jar upside down and propping it up in such a way that the bees can get to the holes in the lid.

In Chapter 8, several methods of capturing bees are discussed wherein the bee tree is not cut down. One of these methods requires that a commercial hive be secured to the side of the tree during the operation. There are several ways to do this. A permanent shelf-like stand can be made and nailed to the tree. However, this may damage the tree and a new stand must be made for each tree. This inconvenience can be avoided by constructing an adjustable bolt-on stand that can be moved from tree to tree.

The stand is basically a square of 2 × 4s that bolts around the tree. The 2 × 4s have extra holes drilled in them so that the stand can be adjusted to different sized trees. On one side of the tree, the 2 × 4s are extra long and they serve as a shelf upon which the stand can be set. The hive rests on two hinged boards that can be adjusted so that the hive will be kept level, even though the frame itself may not be perfectly level. The parts of the hive should be lightly nailed together, and nailed or tied to the frame to keep the hive securely in place in case of heavy winds. It is also advisable to drive one large nail into the tree under each side of the frame as added insurance that the frame won't slip.

4. Old-Timers and Common Scents

The Pedigree of Honey
Does not concern the bee
A clover, any time, to him
Is aristocracy.

EMILY DICKINSON c. 1870s
Nature, LVI

Bee hunting as a sport is relatively new. For many years it was serious business. In many rural areas, bee trees were the main source of sweets upon which the primitive economy depended. In some cases, mountain folks kept bees in log gums or in plank gums, but their methods were primitive and the yields were not high. Besides, for the likes of settlers, trappers, and mountain men, bee gums were often too much trouble to keep. It was easier to go find a bee tree and rob its sweet hoard.

Good bee hunters were and still are highly regarded in such societies. They had a skill that put honey on the table, and maybe even produced a little extra to sell. In her book, *Look Back With Love*, Alberta Hannum recounts some of the obituary entries that were made by one Jacob Carpenter "who lived on Three Mile Creek just under the crest of the Blue Ridge." Jacob was a mountain man who lived and died in the Blue Ridge Mountains, and for a period of more than seventy-five years, ending in 1919, he kept notes on life in the mountains around him. Among other things, he made a brief entry in his notebook every time someone in his mountain community passed away. In that entry he would note what he considered to be some

Cutting bee trees
has long been a method
of obtaining sweets
for the table, as
demonstrated by these
1914 bee hunters in
Kansas. Note the
large porcelain pan in
which to carry
home the bounty.

salient features of the individual's life. When one Soonzy Ollis passed away, Jacob wrote:

> *Soonzy Ollis, age 84*
> *dide June 10, 1871*
> *grates bar hunter & turkies*
> *bee trees by honders and ratel snak by 100*
> *cild deer by thousand*
> *I no him well*

Needless to say, I didn't know old Soonzy. But I wish I had. I'm sure I would have liked him. And I would sure like to know he found those "bee trees by honders." I'll bet that among other things, he relied heavily on scents to attract bees. All the old-timers did. In the next chapter, I will describe what I consider to be the most modern and refined methods of tracking or "coursin'" the bee to his tree. But first let's digress and look at how the old-time bee hunters did it. Some of their techniques are still pretty effective, and the more the bee hunter knows about all the various tricks and techniques of this sport, the better prepared he will be to cope with the infinite number of variations and challenges that crop up when he takes up the tracking of the bee.

BURNING FOR BEES

A favorite trick of the old-time hunters was to "go burnin' for bees." If the hunter were going to burn for bees, he first built a campfire and heated some large flat rocks in it. One of the rocks was then moved far enough away to be out of the smoke and away from the heat of the fire. The bee hunter would place a piece of comb full of honey on the rock, and then the waiting would begin. The heat of the rock would melt

Old-time bee hunters used to attract bees by "burning" for them, and the method is still pretty effective. A rock is heated in a fire, and comb with honey in it is set on the rock to melt. Bees are attracted by the aroma, and soon a beeline will be established.

the comb and cause melted beeswax and hot honey to run over the
rock. Soon the mountain air would be filled with the sweet smell of
hot honey, and bees could detect this smell from surprising distances.
In *Foxfire 2*, the editors quote a veteran Appalachian bee hunter,
Lawton Brooks, on the subject of the smelling (scenting) ability of
bees: "And it's funny, such a scent as they've got. They can smell
anything from miser'ble fur. You can put out a little bait here for one
across up yonder, and he'll come right down to it."

And come right down to it they will. Pretty soon, if there were
any bees in the area, the bee hunter would find the rock with the
honey and beeswax covered with bees. Once the bees had gotten their
fill of honey, they would lift off, circle a few times and make a
"beeline" for their tree. The bee hunter would watch them depart and
attempt to determine the direction in which they were going. Once
determined, he would take another rock, move several hundred yards
down the beeline and repeat the process, and little by little he would
close in on the tree.

I'm sure there have been hundreds and possibly thousands of
bee trees found by this method. There are, however, some disadvantages to the technique. For one thing, flat rocks are not readily
available everywhere and once found, buggy-lugging them all over
the mountains can be quite a chore. For another thing, if the rock is
hot enough to melt the wax and to make the honey give off a good
strong scent, it may be too hot for the bees to land on it. Another
disadvantage of this method is that bees load up very slowly on
undiluted honey, and the hunter must wait, for what seems like an
eternity, for the bees to get a load and depart.

But there is a lesson to be learned from the method, and that
lesson is that the smell of hot honey draws bees like a magnet. If
you ever happen to be out hiking or camping in the woods with no bee
hunting equipment, this method will work with nothing more than a
little honey. Beeswax is not needed.

OTHER SCENTS

Bee hunters have used many scents over the years, but the most
popular is oil of anise. Oil of anise is extracted from the seed of the
anise plant, and it is used in making candies such as licorice. Bees
find the scent of this oil quite attractive, and bee hunters have found
various ways to use it in their hunting.

Some bee hunters sprinkle a little of the scent on their clothing and go for a leisurely stroll in the woods. Supposedly, any bees in

Carrying heated rocks through the woods can be quite a chore, but untold thousands of bee trees have been found by "burnin' fer the bees."

the area will be attracted to the scent and will soon be buzzing around the hunter. The hunter then provides the bees some sugar water (one part sugar, two parts water by volume) and the bees load up. When the bees load up and take off again, the hunter notes the direction of their departure and he is on his way.

A variation on this theme is to sprinkle the anise scent liberally on a piece of cloth and then wave the cloth in the air. This method puts a lot of scent in the air at one time. If the bee hunter is lucky enough to bring in some bees this way, he again feeds them sugar water and notes the direction of their departure. He then travels several hundred yards down the beeline and repeats the process hoping to close in gradually on the tree.

Still another way to use the anise scent is to cut a small leafy branch, sprinkle anise oil on it, and wave it in the air. Once the bees begin to arrive, place a second small branch on top of the first and sprinkle sugar water on the second branch. Soon the bees will be feeding on the sugar water and a beeline can be established, after which the process is repeated further down the beeline. As with the burning method, one of the beauties of this method is the limited

Plastic bottles with built-in stoppers are ideal for carrying bait and scent.

amount of equipment needed—a small bottle of anise scent and a container of sugar water. The forest will provide the leafy branches.

Anise oil, as you buy it in the store, is quite expensive in terms of how much you get for your money. Stated another way, the bottle isn't too expensive, but you probably didn't even know they made bottles that small. However, since the oil has a very strong aroma, it is possible to dilute it considerably and still get satisfactory results. Since the anise extract is an oil, it does not dilute well in water, but I found that the following works well. Put two ounces of water and two ounces of alcohol into a plastic container and mix thoroughly. Add one dram of anise oil and vigorously shake the mixture. The anise oil will mix evenly through the solution, and you will have enough scent to last through an entire active season of bee hunting.

Other oils used by bee hunters as attractive scents include essence of sweet clover and bergamot (also spelled bergamont). These swell smelling scents are used in the same way as the anise scent, and some bee hunters even make mixtures of them.

Many veteran bee hunters feel that the best scent to use to attract bees is a scent made from the plant that the bees are most actively working at the time. To make a scent from any particular flower, such as goldenrod, collect several branches of the flower and carefully separate the flowers from the stems and leaves. Ball the flowers up into a fairly compact mass, put them into the bottom of a

For the scent to be effective, it must be dispersed in the air. A favorite technique of old-timers was to cut some branches, squirt the scent in the branches, and then wave them in the air.

If you leave your scent bottles exposed on your trampings through the woods and fields, you can expect company.

one-pint Mason jar, and add a mixture of one part alcohol to three parts of water deep enough to cover the flowers. Cover the concoction and let it stand for three or four days. Then open the jar, crush and mix the flowers with the blunt end of a stick, and strain the mixture into a vial or a small jar for transport with you into the woods.

A word of caution is in order here in regard to the distinction between baits and scents. Scents are mixtures, such as diluted anise oil, that are intended to attract bees by their aroma. Baits are substances, such as sugar water, that the bee is supposed to ingest and take home. Some bee hunters mix the two so that they only have to take one preparation along with them. Don't do it. For one thing, you will often want pure scent with no sticky water in it to sprinkle on clothing and equipment. For another thing, there is reason to believe that certain of the scents may be harmful to bees if they ingest them. So keep the two separate.

The old time bee hunters lived in rural areas, and much of what they knew about hunting bees they learned from observation of the natural world around them. One of the things they learned was that bees are attracted to salt. They knew that it was not uncommon to find bees on salt licks set out for cattle or at other naturally occurring salt formations (called "licks"). And they knew how to take advantage of this fact.

Bees show the greatest affinity to salt in the early spring. This appears to have something to do with the rearing of brood. The bee hunter would take a shallow pan, put some old corn cobs in it, sprinkle the cobs lightly with salt, and place the pan in a likely spot in the woods. At this point a little scent, such as anise oil, would be added to the sides of the pail or trough to attract any bees that might be flying by. Some hunters would pour water over the cobs immediately, others would leave the pan out and wait for rain to do the job. But whichever method they used, they would periodically check the pan for feeding bees. Once the bees were found, a little scent would be sprinkled in the area, the bees would be fed some sugar water, and then the bee hunter would proceed as though he had brought the bees in with a scent. Some hunters set out several such salt baits, rather than just one, in order to improve their chances of success, and some used hollow logs, depressions in rocks, etc., rather than pans. It is a good idea when using this technique to elevate the baits since many wild animals are attracted to salt and will quickly slurp up the bait if given half a chance.

The old-time bee hunters were colorful characters and, as one would expect, some of them had pretty individualistic and unusual baits. One such bait was a bucket of sand into which the bee hunter urinated and which he then set out into the woods.

"Did it work well?"

"Fer sure it did. Them bee'd jes come a-runnin'."

"And what if there weren't any bees at the bait when you checked it ?"

"Hide jes add a little more scent."

"Oh. And what did you call this device?"

"We-uns aluz called hit stink bait."

Well I've never tried the method and I don't intend to, but I sure wouldn't argue with the name.

OLD-TIMERS ON THE TRAIL

The next chapter describes in detail what I consider to be the most effective ways of tracking bees. These techniques are distilled from my own experiences and from those of other hunters. But the old-timers eschewed these methods. Maybe they hadn't thought of them; maybe they were too dang-fangled complicated; maybe they just wanted to stick with their old ways. Whatever the reasons, they had their old ways and they stuck to them; and one of those ways was "sunnin' the bee."

When a bee lifts off a bait such as honey or sugar water, she circles several times to get her bearings. The bee hunter must visually follow the path of the bee as she circles so that he can see the direction in which she departs. But keeping an eye on the swiftly flying bee is difficult at best, and often the hunter loses sight of her. Over the years, bee hunters found that the bees were easier to see if they were backlighted. Consequently, the bee hunter would situate himself so that the bees he was trying to follow would be between himself and the sun. He would then hold his hat or his hand in front of the sun and get the bee as close to the bright disc of the sun as possible to make it easier to see. As a result of this practice, there are a lot of bee hunters running around in the hills with impaired vision. Don't use this method. There are many safer (and I think more effective) ones described in the next chapter.

One hunting method that the old-timers used was effective and can still be used whenever you get caught in a good hunting location without all of your gear. All it takes is a clear glass tumbler, a piece of dark cloth big enough to cover the tumbler, and some honey or sugar water.

Find a place such as a patch of goldenrod or clover to which

Honey made from the blossoms of the sourwood is the most highly prized of all honeys produced in the United States.

the bees are being naturally attracted. Take the tumbler and slip it over the bee, closing up the open end with your hand (or with a large leaf if you are squeamish). Turn the tumbler upside down, and you will find that the bee will fly upward to the bottom of the tumbler and will be trapped. Sprinkle some diluted honey or sugar water on a large leaf, a flat rock, a board, or other flat surface and place the tumbler down over the baited surface. The bee will continue to buzz around frantically in the upper end (bottom) of the tumbler looking for a means of escape. So how do we get her to come down? That's what the black rag comes in. A trapped bee will instinctively travel upward and will instinctively travel toward the light, but if those two drives are in conflict, she will move toward the light. Cover the tumbler with the dark cloth and allow just a little light to get in around the bottom

edge. The bee will soon travel downward toward the light, still looking for a means of escape. In the course of her explorations around the
bottom of the glass, she will eventually stumble upon the sugar water
and take a sip. And once she tastes it, all thoughts of escape are lost.
She totally forgets her plight. Once you see her drinking the bait, you
can remove the tumbler. She will totally ignore her new-found free-
dom until she has taken on every bit of cargo that she can, at which
time she will lift off, circle a few times, and head for the hive. She will,
of course, return with others to collect the rest of the sugar water, and
if you didn't get a good fix on her direction when she left the bait, you
can get a line on her or one of her friends when they return.

If a bee is trapped in a tumbler, she will instinctively fly toward the top.
If the tumbler is turned upside down over some sugar water or diluted
honey and then covered with a dark cloth, the bee will settle down
and begin to feed. Once the bee has begun feeding, the tumbler can be
removed and the bee will continue to feed. If you are lucky, she will then
fly back to her colony and establish a beeline.

Another old-timers' trick was to carry along some of whatever the bees were foraging on as they moved down the beeline. Generally, the hunter would find a small patch of goldenrod or sumac that the bees were actively working, and he would cut down all but a few plants. These plants would be sprinkled with sugar water and a scented rag would be hung nearby. The bees will show some confusion at first, but soon they will be feeding on the newly provided sweets. Once the bees have become accustomed to working the bait, and the bee hunter has determined the direction of the beeline, the remaining plants are cut down and moved along the beeline several hundred yards. The scent rag is waved around to get some scent into the air to attract the bees, the goldenrod or sumac is laid over the scent rag, the pile is saturated with sugar water, and with a little luck the bees will soon be feeding at the new location.

I said earlier that bee hunting in rural areas was serious business and that was depended upon to provide sweetening for the table. That was only half true. There were, and I suppose may still be, some areas where bee hunting was extremely important business. It may even have been a matter of life and death in some colonial settings. But regardless of the seriousness of the pursuit, it maintains a magnetic appeal to those who have tried it. Again quoting from *Foxfire 2*, four Appalachian mountain men gave their sentiments about bees and bee hunting.

Lawton Brooks: I like t'hunt 'em. If you ever got started t'hunt-in 'em, you'd be a'huntin' em all th' time. It's somethin' t'do.

Lou Reid: I like t'fool with bees. I've worked at these so much that my shoulder'll hurt. I like t'work with 'em though.

Esco Pitts: They're an interestin' thing t'study, a bee is.

Elb McClure: Most interestin' thing you ever seen t'fool with.

And I wouldn't argue with a one of them.

5. Tracking the Bee

Bee hunting combines almost everything that is desirable in a sport. It is played out of doors. It requires the exercise of both the muscles and the brain. It is a sport of brawn and of craft. It can be played alone. Moreover it can be played at any tempo . . . . The sport is one of infinite variety, of suspense, of disappointment, perseverance, and triumph. Your ostensible object is honey. It is the least of your rewards. The reward is when, after hours or days of trial and error, your eye catches the flash of wings in the tree and you are able to say "checkmate". . . .

GEORGE H. EDGELL
The Atlantic Monthly, JULY 1949

Now we get to the real essence of this bee hunting matter. Gathering up the equipment is just a matter of logistics. And once you've found the tree, cutting it down and capturing the bees is just a matter of mechanics. But finding the tree! Therein lies the challenge.

A STARTING POINT

Where do we even begin in our search for the bee tree? In the dense woods? In a farm field? In a park? In our backyard?

The answer to all of those proposed starting points is yes. Any of them will do. It is possible to find honey bees almost anywhere, and that is part of the appeal of the sport. Five of the first six bee trees I found were within the city limits of the small city in which I live. While doing part of the research for this book, I utilized the facilities of a library in the downtown section of the city. On the way into the library one day, I noticed that one of the flowering shrubs in front of the building was covered with honey bees. If I had had the time, I'm sure I could have established a beeline right there in the middle of town and followed those bees back to their tree.

However, notwithstanding the fact that bees can be found almost anywhere, it is true that certain areas offer better chances of success than others. First of all, I would try to avoid an area near any place where bees are being kept by professional or hobby beekeepers. It is very frustrating to spend one or more days on the track of a beeline, only to come up over the rise of a hill and find that your beeline leads to someone's backyard beehive.

By the same token, it is often difficult to get a beeline established in a dense forest of mature trees. In such a forest, the bee pasture will be scant, the bees will be disbursed, they will often be flying over the trees, and it will be hard to get a beeline going. It is always preferable, when possible, to start your beeline from some place where the bees are already foraging. In such cases, it may be possible to establish a beeline and find the tree without ever resorting to scents. If, for example, you can find a patch of clover, goldenrod, or some other plant that the bees are actively using for forage, you can capture some bees in your bait box right there, with no need to try to bring them in with a scent. However, in many cases you won't be so lucky. Often it will seem that no flowers are in bloom anywhere and that the bees have all evaporated. In such a situation, it will be necessary to attract the bees by scenting. But whether you attract the bees with a scent or find them working on plants, the piece of equipment from which the beeline is established is the bait box.

USE OF THE BAIT BOX

Chapter 3 discusses the construction of two types of bait boxes: the traditional shallow box and Donovan's New Improved Vertical Bee Bait Box (hereinafter referred to as the vertical bait box). I will begin by describing the use of the vertical box, since I find it easier to use in most circumstances.

The vertical box is absolutely perfect for use where the bees are foraging on a low lying plant or flower, such as dandelion or white clover. White clover can often be found in the lawns of homes, public buildings, golf courses, and in the trimmed grass along roadsides where, because of the continual cutting, it is kept in constant bloom throughout much of the summer.

Let's assume that you've found a patch of white clover that the bees are actively working, and that you wish to establish a beeline with a vertical bait box. Begin by taking the piece of comb, filling it with sugar water or diluted honey from your bait bottle, and place the comb in the upper compartment of the vertical bait box.

The vertical bait box lends itself readily to the capture of bees that are working on low-lying flowers such as dandelion and some clovers. In such cases, the open end of the box is placed down over the bee, which will then move toward the light in the upper compartment.

Next place a transparent cover over the front opening of the box, and another transparent cover over the top opening. You are now ready to catch your first bee.

To catch a bee, simply walk through the clover until you find a honey bee working on a clover blossom and place the bait box down over her. The bee will be sufficiently engrossed in her nectar gathering activities that you can usually place the box over her with little difficulty.

The design of the box is such that the only light the bee can see is coming from the crack above her (assuming that the box is making fairly good contact with the ground). The natural inclination of a trapped bee is to move upward and toward any light. In five to ten seconds you will see your bee buzzing around excitedly in the upper compartment of the box, looking for an avenue of escape. It is possible to start a beeline with just one bee. However, it is preferable to start with fifteen to twenty. This is because some of the bees wander off or don't return for one reason or another. However, with fifteen to twenty bees in your bait box, you can be relatively assured that a beeline will be established. To capture the additional bees, proceed through the flower patch placing the bait box over one bee after another. After the first few bees have been caught, the confusion in the upper compartment will be such that it will be impossible to tell when the bee you are trying to capture has joined those in the upper compartment. The solution is to leave the box over the bee for twenty to thirty seconds, which is enough time for the average bee to make her way to the upper compartment. If you raise the box too quickly and the bee has not yet made her way up the box, she will fly off to the nearest flower and continue her work. Bees really don't get very excited about such goings-on.

Once you have captured an adequate number of bees, you are ready for step two. If you look through the transparent front cover, you will notice that most of the bees are still buzzing excitedly at the front window trying to escape. Few, if any, will have settled down to drink the sugar water in the comb. To remedy this situation, place the bait box on the ground, and place the wooden covers over the front and top windows. The wooden covers will darken the upper chamber and cause the bees to calm down. In the darkness, the bees will explore their cage looking for a way out, they will discover the sugar water, and they will load up. Leave the upper chamber dark for four or five minutes. In this length of time most of the bees will have filled up with sugar water or will be filling up. After the four or five minutes have elapsed, you are ready to release the bees and establish a beeline. But before discussing the beeline, it is worth considering what one does if the bees are scarce, or if they are working on tall plants or weeds where the box cannot simply be placed down over them.

When the bees are working tall forage, getting the bees into the box is a little more of an exercise. But if the bees are plentiful, it should still be possible to capture fifteen or twenty bees in fifteen minutes. Walk carefully through the forage, shaking the plants as little as possible. When a bee is spotted working near the top of a

When bees are being
captured in the vertical
bait box, both the
front and top openings
should be covered with a
transparent material.
Once the bees are
captured, both openings
should be covered
with an opaque material,
which will darken the
upper chamber and cause
the bees to discover
the sugar water.
To release the bees,
take both covers
off the upper opening.

plant or in some other readily accessible place on the plant, lower the box slowly toward the bee while at the same time bringing a small piece of wood (just big enough to cover the bottom of the box) up underneath the bee. When the board and the box are four to six inches from closing on the bee, quickly slap the two together and the bee will be securely trapped in the bottom chamber. Hold the box upright and, as before, give the bee ten or fifteen seconds to move up into the upper chamber. Continue this process until you have fifteen or twenty bees and then darken the upper chamber to stimulate the bees to feed.

If the bees are scarce, it will be necessary to use a scenter to bring them in. To do this, fill the comb with sugar water and place it in the bait box, but do not put any covers over the front or top openings. Hang the bait box at an elevation of two or three feet and

When using the vertical bait box on tall plants, a piece of wood is needed to cover the bottom opening. The box and the piece of wood are brought into position around the bee, and when they are about six inches apart they slapped together, trapping the bee inside.

set up a scenting device on the ground under the box. A stick about three feet long with a fork in one end and sharpened at the other end makes a convenient stand for the bait box. Just push the sharpened end into the ground and hang the bait box in the fork by its handle.

Warm honey is so effective at attracting bees that they seem to materialize out of thin air. One way to heat the honey is with a scent can like the ones described in Chapter 3. Fill the honey cup with honey, light the candle, and adjust the height of the cup so that the honey is brought to a slow boil. Soon the air will be filled with the smell of boiling honey. One of the greatest thrills for a bee hunter is to be sitting in a remote field or woodlot on a lazy summer day with his scent can working and hear the whining buzz of an incoming bee. The bee will circle about and hover around the scent can. She will dart away. Will she come back or is she gone? Then she comes back. Then she spots the white of the bait box and is attracted. She hovers. She circles. She investigates. Then she lands on the comb and begins to feed. The beeline is started!

The method just described for attracting bees involved the use of the scent can. The honey could, of course, have been heated using the alternate equipment described in Chapter 3. You could even "burn" for them as described in the previous chapter. The method employed is not important, so long as it gets the smell of hot honey into the air.

In lieu of honey, you could also use any of the scents described in Chapter 4. Just sprinkle a little of the scent on a piece of cloth and wave the cloth in the air a few times. This will get the scent into the air. Then hang the cloth near your bait box and have a seat. And wait. And watch. And listen. And if you are lucky, before too long you will be rewarded by the whine of approaching wings.

ESTABLISHING THE BEELINE

Whether you captured the bees directly in your bait box or brought them in with scents, you should now have one or more filled up bees in your bait box and those bees should be about ready to head back to their hive. If the bees were captured and are in the darkened upper chamber, it is time to release them. To do so, remove the cover from the top hole of the bait box. When you remove the cover, about half of the bees will come spilling out in the first few seconds and the rest, some of whom may still be lapping up sugar water, will follow shortly. You need not fear being stung as the bees exit. When loaded up with sugar water or honey, they are quite docile. The only thing on a bee's mind as she exits the bait box is getting home with her cargo of sweets.

Observe closely the behavior of the bees as they leave the bait box and head back to the hive. The bee will take off from the bait box and start flying in circles around the box. The circles will get larger and larger and higher and higher as she goes. The bee does this to fix the location of the bait in her mind and to get her bearings with respect to the course she must fly to get back to her colony. After circling anywhere from two or three to seven or eight times, the bee is satisfied that she has her bearings and heads off in a straight line (beeline) for the bee tree. Note well the direction of the bee's departure and line it up with some prominent terrain feature such as a tree or a building, for it is along that line that the bee tree lies.

The foregoing description would probably lead you to believe that establishing a beeline is a fairly simple matter and, in fact, if you are an experienced bee hunter, it's not too difficult. There are, however, some problems and subtleties that may not be apparent at first blush. For example, when the bees come tumbling out of the box, it is tough to keep your eye on just one of them as they circle and criss-cross in your field of view. It is not at all uncommon for a beginner to find that one moment he has eight or ten bees whizzing around in circles in front of him and the next moment he has none and that he has failed to get a beeline on a single bee. If this happens, watch for successive bees coming out of the box. If you start with fifteen or twenty bees, they will not all come out and take off at once. Some will still be in the box drinking sugar water. Others will manage to get sugar water all over themselves and they will sit on the outside of the bait box for what seems like an eternity rubbing their legs and cleaning themselves before taking off. If you fail to establish a beeline with the first bees out of the box, you may be able to do so with one of these laggards.

There are other difficulties attendant to marking the flight of the bee. The most serious difficulty is that it just isn't easy to follow with the human eye the circular flight pattern of an insect that is 3/8" long and is zipping along at ten to twenty miles per hour. Often as the bee is circling, you will lose it. You will follow its first few circles and then lose it in the sun. Or it will circle behind you before you can turn around. Or it will fly against a background that offers too little contrast. Or you will blink. Or it will just vanish into thin air. But that's another reason for starting with fifteen or twenty bees; the chances are that you will lose sight of many of them.

It is much easier to mark the flight of the bee in an open area such as a field or a lawn. In wooded areas, or even on lawns and in parks where there are trees nearby, it is very easy to lose the bee as she circles. This is partially due to the fact that the bee will not stand out well against the uneven texture of leaves, branches, and trunks and in part to the fact that the bee will often disappear behind, into, or over the tree. It is best to find a spot that is free of trees in all directions for at least 100 feet. Often this is not possible. In heavy forest you should look for the best clearing or opening you can find, and clear out as much brush and small growth as you can to open up the area and to make spotting the bee easier.

I find that I frequently lose sight of bees as they circle in front of the sun, and thus I tend to favor overcast days for bee hunting. If the day is sunny, try to position yourself with your back to the sun facing the bait box, and far enough away from the box that you won't have to turn and look into the sun as the bee circles. Another useful trick is to get as close to the ground as possible, even lying on your back as necessary so that you will be spotting the bee against the sky. The black speck of the bee is much easier to spot against the sky than it is against the broken background texture of plants, tree, rocks, buildings, etc.

You will quickly come to note an interesting fact about the circles that the bee flies around the bait box. The first few circles will be directly around the box itself. However, as the circles get bigger and bigger, they will often tend to drift in such a way that while the circle still encloses the bait box, the box is no longer at the center of the circle. In my experience, the direction of drift invariably indicates the direction of the tree. Trying to determine the direction of the beeline in this manner is not nearly as accurate as actually seeing the bee take off on the beeline, but it is an indicator.

Sometimes you will be lucky with the bees that you release and you will obtain a positive beeline with them. However, more often than not you will find that all you got was an estimate as to the direction of the beeline. Or maybe you brought the bees in to the bait with scent and only had one or two bees to begin with. If that was the case, it is now that the waiting begins.

The bees that have left the bait box will normally return to their colony and tell the other workers what they have found. They will then return to the bait bringing one or two more workers with them. Sometimes they will return alone for the next few trips and not bring others until they are sure of the source. But usually within half an hour to an hour there will be a steady stream of bees working the bait.

These photos are a timed sequence that illustrates how quickly the
number of bees working the bait will build up. The first bee is attracted
by a scent and alights at time zero. Five minutes later there are two bees
on the bait. Fifteen minutes after the first bee landed there are so many
bees on the bait that other bees are stacked up over the box looking
for a place to land. The bait box in these pictures was approximately
100 yards from the bee tree.

But sometimes none will return. Why? Who knows. If you
only started with one or two bees, maybe they fell prey to birds. Or
maybe they lost track of the location of the bait. Or maybe they were
distracted by some other source of forage. But that very uncertainty
is the source of much of the excitement of bee hunting. You release
the bees and wait. Will they return? Five minutes pass. Nothing. Ten
minutes. Nothing. Eleven and twelve. You begin to think that you
may have struck out. And then you hear the whirr of wings and see the
glint of sunlight off the yellow body. The next thing you know you
have a hovering bee standing motionless in midair just off the bait.
Success! The bees are returning.

There are several reasons for wanting to get the bees to
return to the bait, rather than just trying to establish the beeline
with the initial release of bees. The most obvious reason, of course, is
that you may not have been able to determine the beeline from the
initial group of bees. As more and more bees begin working the bait, it
becomes easier and easier to determine the course of the bees. Not
only do the increased numbers of bees make spotting easier, but also
as the bees become more familiar with the location of the bait they
will circle it fewer times as they depart. On occasion you will find a
jewel of a bee who will be so intent on getting back to the colony that
she will hardly circle at all, but will head straight for home. Such bees
are particularly useful in close cover where you often lose sight of the
bees as they circle. But the bees won't leave the bait and fly directly

back to the tree without circling until they have made the trip several times. Some will continue to circle regardless of how many times they have made the trip.

Another reason for wanting the bees to return from the colony and begin to work the bait is that once they have started working the bait, you can time a bee's round trip and get some idea of how far you are from the bee tree.

In order to time the bee's round trip, it is necessary to mark a bee in some way so that you can distinguish her from the others. Placing a mark on a bee may put you in mind of the children's story about the mice that wanted to tie a bell on the cat so they could hear the cat approaching. All the mice thought it was a great idea, but none wanted to volunteer to do the tying. Putting a mark on a bee sounds like a great idea, but you may be less than enthusiastic about doing it. You will be even less enthusiastic when I tell you that it's done with a paint brush.

All that you need in the way of equipment to mark the bee is a piece of chalk and a small artist's-type paint brush. Once the bees are well established working the bait, scrape a little chalk dust loose from the piece of chalk, moisten it with saliva, dip in the paint brush and select a bee that appears to be particularly engrossed in drinking up the sugar water. Take your moistened brush and give the targeted bee a swipe or two across the topside of her abdomen. If you can find a bee that is buried in one of the cells of honeycomb up to her shoulders,

When timing the round-trip flight of a bee, it is necessary to mark the bee in some way so that it can be distinguished from other bees. This is done by dabbing the bee with a paint brush dipped in moist chalk dust.

so much the better. Such a bee is so totally immersed in her work that you could paint the Mona Lisa on her without complaint.

The chalk mark doesn't affect the marked bee and it goes unnoticed by her fellow workers. Watch the marked bee, and when she takes off, note the time of her departure. The chalk mark is surprisingly durable, and you will have no trouble spotting the tagged worker when she returns. Note the time of her return and determine the time for the round trip. The distance from the hive to the bait can then be approximately determined using this round trip time. This determination is somewhat inexact because of some uncertainties in the bee's trip. One uncertainty is the speed of the bee's flight. Loaded bees average between thirteen and sixteen miles per hour and unloaded bees (those leaving the colony and returning to the bait) average between seven and twenty-nine miles per hour. On the average, loaded bees travel at about fifteen miles per hour and unloaded bees at thirteen miles per hours. Another uncertainty is introduced into the calculation by the length of time that the bee spends in the tree. The worker bee will unload her cargo in one to two minutes. But one can never be sure how far she had to crawl in the tree to get to the point where she could unload. It is safe to say, though, that from the time that the worker enters the tree until she leaves probably averages two to four minutes for most trees, and an average of three minutes is probably not too far off.

Using the above average figures for flight speed and unloading time in the tree, it is possible to construct the following table.

DISTANCE (MILES)	TIME (MINUTES)
1/4	5.2
1/2	7.3
3/4	9.5
1	11.6

For times greater than 11.6 minutes, add ¼ mile for every 2.2 minutes. But don't be very optimistic about finding the tree if the round trip takes the bee more than fifteen minutes. In such cases, most bee hunters just pick up and relocate.

Sometimes, especially when the bee hunter is in heavy timber, it can be frustratingly difficult to determine the direction in which the bees are going. One bee after another will circle and seem to disappear. In such circumstances, there are several tricks that the bee hunter can employ to improve his chances of accurately determining the beeline. If the bees are working the bait heavily and there are a lot of arrivals and departures, one thing the hunter can do is to look for arriving bees rather than watch departing bees. The incoming bees will usually be flying a little slower, but even more important, they will be coming in on a straight line until they get very near the bait box, at which point they begin to circle. Thus if the bee hunter moves a few yards away from the bait and looks for incoming bees, especially if he can get them silhouetted against the sky, he may be able to determine the beeline from arrivals rather than departures.

Another trick is to listen for the bees. If the bees are not rising too rapidly from the bait, it is possible to hear them flying in and out. Walk around the bait in a circle of about ten yards in radius and you may hear your beeline before you see it.

At this point you should also beware of a potential pitfall. In

When releasing bees from the bait box, it is usually best to stand back from the box. You are more likely to lose sight of the bees if you stand near the box.

trying to get your beeline established, you may become confused because the bees appear to be flying off in several directions. Such a turn of events is no cause for concern or frustration. Quite the contrary. It probably means that you have established a course to two or more colonies. It is quite common for bees from two or more colonies to be foraging in the same area. Note the direction of each beeline and start by working the strongest line, i.e., the one that has the most bees.

HOW TO WORK THE BEELINE

Once the beeline is established, the question arises of what to do with it. The hunter's first impulse is to go charging off examining every tree along the beeline in the hopes of finding the honey tree. But hold on just a minute. To begin with, the beeline is never exact. No two bees will return to the colony along *exactly* the same line. If there is an obstacle such as a tall tree in the bees' line of flight, one bee will go around it to the right, another will go to the left, and the third will lift up and fly over it. So you may think that you have the beeline exactly determined, but practically speaking, the true line could well be five or ten degrees to either side of your hypothetical line. If the bees are coming from a tree three quarters of a mile to a mile away, and the area is fairly wooded, you will quickly discover that there are a lot of trees in the ten to twenty degree sector in front of you. In such a case, it is necessary to get a better fix on the location of the tree. There are three ways to do this: relocation of the bait box; introduction of a second bait box; and intersection.

The best time to relocate the bait box is when you have a strong course of bees working the bait. Wait until you have a large number of bees in the box, preferably ten to twenty, and then put the transparent covers over the top hole and the front opening. This will trap the bees inside. If you are going to travel over rough terrain, or delay for more than a few minutes in getting the box to its new location, you should also cover the bottom opening.

Once the bees are trapped, move along the direction of the beeline a distance of three or four hundred yards, set the bait box back up, and remove both transparent covers to release the bees. The bees will leave the box, circle about, and head for the tree. Do not place too much confidence in the direction taken by this first release of bees since they will probably be somewhat confused and may not get back to their tree along a very straight route. What the bee hunter is counting on when he relocates the bait box is that the bees will reestablish the beeline. If you are successful, you should know within twenty minutes. If the bees have not returned within twenty minutes, they probably aren't going to. One reason for failure to reestablish the beeline could be that you have gone past the bee tree. If the beeline is not reestablished at the new location, go back to the previous location, catch another load of bees, and this time only move half as far along the beeline as you did previously. Release the bees and again try to get the bees to work the bait. It is sometimes useful in such circumstances to boil a little honey or to use some other scenting technique to attract the bees to the new bait box location.

If you have two or more bait boxes, another technique that is useful in refining the beeline is to leave the first bait box in place, move down the beeline several hundred yards, and set up a second bait box. If your determination of the beeline is accurate, there will surely be bees flying by overhead or in the general area as they fly back and forth from the tree to the first bait box. Once the second box is set up at the new location, use one of the scenting techniques

described in the previous chapter to attract the bees. Since they are
flying right by the new location on their way back and forth from the
established bait box, it is a relatively easy matter to intercept them
and divert them to the new box by using an attractive scent. The
advantage is that once the beeline is set up on the new bait box, you
will be several hundred yards closer to the tree. Once you are sure
that the bees are actively working the box in the new location, you
can go to the previous location, seal up the bait box with any bees that
happen to be feeding in it, and relocate that box still closer to the tree.
Using this technique it is possible to "leapfrog" one's way to the tree.

A third method of refining the beeline is intersection. the
method, though not exact, is very useful at times. To employ this
technique, first establish a beeline from your bait box as previously
described. Then, using the same bait box or a different one, move 200
to 400 yards to one side of the beeline (do not move down the beeline
toward the tree). At this new location, establish a second beeline. The
tree will be located at approximately the point where this latter
beeline intersects the one previously established. This technique is
useful where heavy wood cover or other obstacles make it difficult to
move down the original beeline and establish new bait box locations.
This method can also be used in conjunction with the timing technique previously described to estimate the distance to the tree.

This intersection method of locating the bee tree is an old one,
and it is described in the oldest known English language article about
bee hunting. The Honorable Paul Dudley described this technique in
the January-February-March-April 1721 issue of the *Philosophical
Transactions of the Royal Society of London*. The article was printed
under the following heading:

VII An Account of a Method
lately found out in New-England
for Discovering where the Bees
Hive in the Woods, in order
to get their Honey.

Mr. Dudley then went on to describe what he considered to be
the general method of establishing a beeline.

The hunter in a clear Sun-shining day, takes a Plate or Trencher,
with a little sugar, Honey, or Molasses spread on it, and when got into
the woods, sets it down on a Rock or a Stump in the Woods: this the
Bees soon scent and find out: for 'tis generally supposed a Bee will
scent Honey or Wax above a Mile's distance.

Interesting, but I don't think I would want to waste too much time sitting in the woods watching a plate of sugar and waiting for the bees to start feeding on it. For one thing, the bees are unlikely to smell it without assistance from some other scent, and for another thing, conditions have to be just right for bees to eat dry sugar. Mr. Dudley goes on to cite the case of a bee hunter who located a bee tree by the intersection method, and who was so sure that it was the bee tree that he cut it down even though he could not see any openings in the tree nor any bees going in or out. Furthermore, he was so sure that he had the right tree that before cutting the tree down he wagered with two companions to the effect that he had the right tree. And according to Mr. Dudley, our confident (impetuous? foolish?) bee hunter won his bet. I sure would like to have met that fellow. He was either the best bee hunter or the biggest fool in the American colonies. My beelines give me the general direction of the tree. But I've never established one that was so good that it led me to the exact tree, let alone two that were so good that they gave me the exact tree by intersection. Once you get the beeline established and know the aproximate location of the tree, you have to start searching. And that brings us to our next topic.

SEARCHING FOR THE TREE

Once the bee hunter thinks he is close enough to the tree to insure himself that he is not looking for a needle in a haystack, it is time to begin in earnest the search for the bee tree. Every bee hunter has his pet ideas about how to look for the tree, what kind of trees are most likely to contain bees, and where on the tree to look for the opening the bees are using (the bee hole).

Some bee hunters say that light-colored bees come from hard-woods and the dark-colored ones come from pines where they are discolored by the sap and resins in the tree. Others maintain that if the bees leave the bait and circle high before leaving, the hole in the bee tree is high, whereas if they just rise a few feet off the bait and zip for home the hole in the tree is low. My experience has been that the color of the bee is determined more by the age and the breed of the bee than it is by the type tree it lives in, and how high the bee rises off the bait is determined by weather, local terrain features, etc., rather than by where the opening is in the tree.

The reader may find the following tabulation to be of some interest. The table, 5-1, provides selected data on the last six bee trees that I have found. I was going to make the table longer, but I

The moment of success for the bee hunter comes when he finds the opening in the tree with the bees spilling in and out. Here are three such openings. Every one was in a hollow but live tree. The openings ranged from two to twenty feet above the ground.

was stung taking measurements on number seven, so you will have to settle for six.

NO.	TREE TYPE	DIAMETER AT BREAST HEIGHT (INCHES)	DEAD?	HEIGHT OF BEE HOLE (FEET)
1	Yellow Pine	18.1	Yes	Ground level
2	Grey Birch	19.4	No	2
3	Walnut	25.1	No	10
4	Willow	43.9	No	20
5	Ash	36.0	No	Ground level
6	Oak	32.5	No	25

I think that this table is fairly representative, and although some features of such a table will vary from place to place around the country, it does allow one to draw certain conclusions. First, note that only one of the six trees was dead when I found it, and even that one may have been alive when the bees colonized it. Maybe the bees have some way of knowing that live trees are more secure homes than dead ones, and maybe they colonize selectively. Maybe there are just more standing hollow trees in the woods that are alive than are dead. Whatever the reason, I have found many more colonies in live trees than in dead ones.

Another interesting point in the table is the size of trees. I have heard reports of trees ten to twelve inches in diameter that contained strong bee colonies and lots of honey, but I have never found one. My experience has been that trees less than eighteen inches in diameter are not likely to contain bees, and the best bet are trees in the range of two and a half to four or five feet. I may have walked past some small bee trees in my day because of this philosophy, but I expect that I have also saved a lot of time. In many areas there simply aren't many trees in the range of two and a half to five feet and the few there are can be examined quickly. If nothing is turned up, smaller trees can be examined.

Note also the variety of species represented in the table. Bees don't seem to show much preference for one type of tree over another, and any large hollow tree will do. It is true, however, that in each part of the country there are certain species of trees that are more likely to grow to the required dimensions and to develop the hollow body cavities that are attractive to bees. For example, throughout much of the South and Southeast, the black gum is a common home for wild bees and it is this fact that has given rise to the practice of referring to bee trees in general as bee gums. Another common bee tree in the South and on the west coast is the live oak. This tree, when allowed to grow to maturity, achieves a large diameter and frequently develops large hollow cavities in the trunk. Where I live in Virginia, the same is true of other oaks such as the black oak and the white oak. On the other hand, you soon come to learn that certain types of trees rarely develop the hollow centers needed for a bee tree. For example, tulip poplars, even those that are eighteen to twenty-four inches in diameter, rarely have hollow centers and only the biggest trees (over three feet in diameter) are really likely to be hollow.

When examining the tree, be sure to check it from all sides. I recall the day that I found tree number 3 in the preceding table. I was following a beeline and saw the tree up ahead of me. As soon as I saw it I thought, "Aha! I found it." It was a big old gnarled tree, still alive, and even from where I stood I could see two holes in the side of the tree where branches had broken off and the stumps had rotted out leaving openings. Those holes appeared to connect with a larger hollow in the trunk of the tree. I rushed up to the tree and examined the holes only to find to my disappointment that there wasn't a bee in sight. I looked up and down the trunk. No bees anywhere. I was about to give up and head on to the next tree when it occurred to me that this tree was such a likely candidate that it really deserved to be inspected from the other side. I wasn't really eager to do so since the ground behind the tree broke off sharply toward a creek and the steep slope was covered with a tangle of brush and green-briar. But I decided to take a look anyway, and it was a good thing that I did. When I finally fought my way around to the other side, there it was—the bee hole. About ten feet above the ground the bees were just streaming in and out of the tree, and the route they were using was such that branches and vines made it hard to see them from the other side of the tree. When looking for the bee hole, start by examining the base of the tree. Many trees rot in such a way that there will be an opening near the roots that connects with the hollow trunk. Bees frequently use these openings. Continue your examination up the trunk looking for splits, woodpecker holes, limb stumps, and other openings that might connect with the trunk. On very large trees with branches a foot or more in diameter, the bees may actually be living in a hollow branch, or may be using a hollow branch for access to the trunk. If the weather is warm, there will be a lot of activity at the hole and the bees will be easy to spot. If the trees are very tall, a pair of binoculars will help, but usually they are not necessary. When checking the higher elevations of big trees, you will frequently be momentarily fooled by various insects that dart around in the tree tops. If you don't spend a lot of time peering intently up the trunks of large trees, and I expect that most folks don't, then you probably don't realize just how many bugs are flitting around up there. With a little practice, you will be able to distinguish those bugs from honey bees and none of them will maintain the continuous flow in and out of the tree that bees do.

TRACKING BEES FROM WATER

It is late July as I write this, and it has been an incredibly wet summer. The ground is soggy. The black leaf spot has wiped out my roses and blue leaf mold is playing havoc with the local tobacco crop. Usually by this time of year it's so dry that I don't have to mow my lawn any more; I just walk around on it and snap the grass off. By August it's normally so dry around here that the ground shrivels and cracks. And in weather that's dry, honey bees have to go out looking for water.

The bees use the water to thin the food that is being fed to brood and to cool the hive by evaporation. When the ground is wet and rainfall is frequent, there are enough scattered pools and casual watering holes that the bees have no trouble finding water. It is rare in such circumstances to find bees concentrating around watering spots. However, as summer progresses and the ground gets drier and drier, one puddle after another disappears. Some of the small creeks also dry up. Gradually the bees have to make more and more of an effort to find water. When this happens, you can find bees collecting

When the summer turns dry, honey bees start to gather water to cool
the hive and to dilute honey being fed to brood. The bee hunter can
capture bees at water and begin his hunts from there.

water at leaky outside faucets on houses and at dripping water fountains in parks. The bee hunter who knows how to do it can take advantage of these facts.

Begin by walking along a small stream, a marshy area, a farm pond, or some other source of water in what would otherwise be a dry area. Keep an eye out for bees taking on water. Once some bees are found, take a position where you can observe them upon take-off. As when they lift off from bait, the bees will rise, circle a few times, and head for their tree. If the bees have been using the watering spot for some time, they may circle very little and head back almost directly to the tree. This makes it much easier on the bee hunter since it is easy to lose sight of the bee while it is circling.

If there are not enough bees working the watering spot, you can establish a good strong course using your bait box. Fill up the comb with sugar water, put the transparent covers on the top and front of the box, and put the box down over one or more bees that are taking on water. From there on, proceed as described in the previous section, and track the bees from the course they set up from the bait box.

One advantage of tracking bees from watering spots is that they gather water from the closest possible sources to their tree. The bee hunter who tracks bees from water often has only a short way to go, and some veteran bee hunters swear by this technique. Of the bee trees listed in Table 5.1, all but tree number 5 were found within fifty yards of a creek, and two of the six trees were growing right on the bank and had exposed roots protruding into the creek bed.

OLD-FASHIONED BAIT BOXES

Earlier in this chapter I described the basic method of tracking bees using a bait box. The method that was described included use of the improved or vertical bait box. There is a second type of bait box, the horizontal or cigar box type, that is popular with some bee hunters. The horizontal bait box is a shallow box three inches wide by six inches long by three inches deep that is divided into two compartments approximately three inches by three inches. The front compartment of the box has a hinged lid with a transparent window in the lid and with some means of covering the window to darken the compartment. The rear compartment has no hinged lid but does have a window that can be darkened. A small hole connects the two compartments, and that hole can be opened or closed from outside the box by means of a sliding strip of wood. Construction details are given

Once a piece of comb is placed in the front compartment of the old-style bait box, some sugar water should be squirted into the comb before the bees are allowed to move into the front compartment.

in Chapter 3. When using this type of bait box, it is also helpful to have a three or four-foot-long piece of broom handle, sharpened on one end, with a six-inch square piece of wood nailed to the other end. The sharp end of the broom handle is pushed into the ground and the wooden square serves as a platform upon which to rest the bait box.

To use this type of bait box, start with no honeycomb in the front compartment, with the window on the front compartment covered, and with the window on the back compartment uncovered. Open the lid on the front compartment. Find a honey bee that is working a blossom, bring the box up under the bee, shake her into the front compartment, and quickly shut the lid. It sounds difficult, but with a little practice it is fairly easy. It may also sound dangerous and you may be thinking, "What if I don't get the bee in the box? Won't it sting me?" The answer is no, the bee won't sting you. If you fail to get it into the box, it will fly off to another flower and continue its work.

Once the bee is in the front compartment, cover the transparent lid on the front compartment and move the slide so as to open the hole connecting the two compartments. Since the front compartment is dark and the window on the rear compartment is uncovered, the bee will see the light coming from the hole to the rear compartment and will quickly walk back into the rear. Give the bee about thirty seconds to get into the rear compartment, then move the slide to close the hole connecting the compartments. You now have one trapped bee.

This process can be repeated over and over until you have ten to twenty bees in the rear compartment, and you are ready to start the beeline. When you feel you have enough bees trapped in the rear compartment, open the lid to the front compartment, drop in a piece of honey comb, and sprinkle it with sugar water or diluted honey. Close the lid and uncover the window on the front compartment. Cover the window on the rear compartment and move the slide so as to open the hole connecting the two compartments. The bees will now find themselves in a dark compartment (the rear one), but they will see light coming from the connecting hole. What will they do? They will take O.J. Simpson's advice and run for the daylight. Once you have as many bees in the front compartment as you want, close the slide.

It is interesting to note the behavior of the bees at this point. Even though there is now honeycomb covered with sugar water in the front compartment, most of them will ignore it and will concentrate on the lighted window looking for a way to escape. As with the vertical bait box, this problem is rectified by covering the front window and once again placing the bees in darkness. During this time, the bees will explore their prison, find the sugar water you have placed in there for them, and start loading up. After four or five minutes, gently open the lid to the front compartment and you are on your way to setting up a beeline. If you still have some bees in the rear compartment, you can repeat the release procedure until all the bees have been released. Then the waiting begins, and the bee hunter strains to hear the whirr of silver wings and to see the flashing gold body of a returning bee.

6. Some Typical Hunts

Winnie-the-Pooh sat down at the foot of the tree, put his head between his paws and began to think.

First of all he said to himself: "That buzzing-noise means something. You don't get a buzzing-noise like that, just buzzing and buzzing, without its meaning something. If there's a buzzing-noise, somebody's making a buzzing-noise, and the only reason for making a buzzing-noise that I know of is because you're a bee."

Then he thought another long time, and said: "And the only reason for being a bee that I know of is making honey."

A.A. MILNE,
The World of Pooh

The bee hunter is a detective. He puts together bits and pieces of information and tries to track down his quarry. Newcomers to the sport of bee hunting occasionally ask how long all this detective work takes. How long will it take them to find a bee tree? After years of research and much exhaustive study involving my own experience and the experience of others, I am happy to report that the answer to that question is finally available. It takes somewhere between twenty-two minutes and three years to find the bee tree.

Why so much variation? Sometimes you will get lucky and start right near the bee tree. Sometimes you will be in fairly open terrain with only a few trees that need to be checked. And sometimes the bees will set up such a strong course that following them is as easy as walking down a sidewalk. On the other hand, sometimes you will get started on a weak course looking for a bee tree that is a mile away through dense forest, where you lose sight of the bees once they get more than ten feet away from the bait. If you are especially unlucky, you'll be getting bees from two different colonies and not know it, the bees will be living in a rock formation while you are checking trees, and for some reason they won't be following a straight line home.

Figuring out where the colony is located in such circumstances is almost as tough as figuring out how to fill out your income tax form. Almost, but not quite.

To give you a feel for the kind of detective work that is required to hunt down the bee tree, I thought it would be helpful to recount some actual bee hunting experiences. Hunts can range from incredibly simple to frustratingly tough, as the following examples indicate.

THE CASE OF THE NOISY GARBAGE CAN

Metal garbage cans can be awfully noisy, especially in the hands of my garbage men. They are absolute virtuosos amongst garbage musicians. One slams the can against the truck and into the sidewalk like he was beating on a kettle drum, while the other keeps time with two metal lids in the fashion of cymbals. It's a real pleasure to watch and listen to masters at work.

But undisturbed garbage cans, even metal ones, are usually pretty quiet. They just sort of sit there minding their own business and hardly ever whimper or say a word. That's why I got curious one day when I heard one buzzing.

My wife and I and our two children had gone into town to see a photographer to have some family pictures taken. As I was holding the door for the family to go into the studio, I thought I heard a buzzing sound behind me like the droning of wings. Most curious. I turned around to investigate and found that then noise was coming from a garbage can sitting on the sidewalk. Curiouser and curiouser. Could it be that a colony had taken up residence right in a garbage can? Maybe a swarm had settled in within the last few days. It was a metal can with one of those roof-like plastic covers with a swinging flap in it, and there was enough clearance around the flap that bees could get by it. And that's just what they were doing—streaming in and out of the can through cracks and openings in the plastic top.

One would not want to get stung on the face just before getting his picture taken, but the temptation was more than I could stand. I carefully pushed back the lid of the can and peered inside. There was no swarm or colony inside, and the can was nearly empty. But it wasn't quite empty. There was only one thing in there to attract the bees, a spilled can of soda pop. Someone had thrown a half a can of soda into the garbage can and the pop had spilled all over the bottom of the can. The bees were in there just lapping it up. It was March, the spring honey flow had not yet begun in earnest, and in the meantime the bees were finding that sweet soda pop was very much to their liking.

At just that moment I was informed by my wife that I was holding everyone up and I was requested to puh-leeze get inside. The female of the species can be so intolerant when it comes to the finer things in life like bee hunting, bass fishing, and lying in the back yard watching the clouds go by when the lawn needs mowing.

After the picture taking, I dallied on the way out long enough to get some sort of beeline on the bees leaving the can. They appeared to be flying across a parking lot immediately adjacent to the building and across a semiopen field beyond. Since I was all gussied up in my Sunday-goin'-to-meetin' clothes and had my better half in tow, I was in no position to take up the hunt then and there. So I rushed home, changed clothes, picked up a few pieces of bee hunting gear, and zipped back to the garbage can accompanied by an eager son and daughter.

Normally I would have set up a bait box right at the can, established a good beeline, captured a few bees, and then moved further down the beeline. But the garbage can that the bees were working was right next to the door of the building, and more people were streaming in and out of the building than there were bees going in and out of the can. I had a feeling that setting up a bait box, establishing a heavy course, and bringing even more bees into the area just might attract a little more attention and create a little more disturbance than I wanted. So how to proceed?

We had already determined that the beeline seemed to go across the parking lot and into the field beyond. By taking a position in the parking lot we were able to pick up the bees flying back and forth overhead and to thereby further refine the beeline. Since the area was open, we were actually able to chase on foot some of the bees that were returning to the tree, and to keep up with them for short distances. Once we had followed the beeline to the edge of the field, and determined its direction as best we could by this method, it was time to proceed to step two.

The field was about 300 yards wide and it sloped gradually down to a creek along which a woodlot began on the far side. We knew the approximate line along which the bees crossed the field, so we followed that line until we were about in the middle of the field. By setting up on the middle of the field, we could minimize the number of trees and buildings near the bait and thus make it easier to follow the bees visually as they left the bait. Since there were no flowering plants in the field at this time of year, there were no bees. Our problem became one of enticing some bees out of the beeline that they were flying overhead and down to our bait. In other words, we had to get a bee that was headed for the soda pop in the garbage can and divert her down to our bait instead.

To do this, we boiled some honey to establish a scent. I had brought along a butane backpacker's lantern which we lit, and we dribbled some honey on the hot metal cover. Soon the air was filled with the sweet smell of hot honey. I knew it wasn't critical that we be right under the beeline, since the smell of the honey would cover a pretty large area and would bring in bees from 50 to 100 yards or more away. My bait boxes were in service elsewhere, so I had to improvise with a plastic can lid about six inches in diameter which I laid out on the ground and into which I sprinkled some diluted honey.

It didn't take long. After about ten minutes the first bee appeared and then another and another. We were unusually lucky this time and got a good line on two of the first few bees that left, and therefore we didn't have to wait for the bees to start working the bait heavily. I had not brought any marking equipment with me so I couldn't mark and time the bees, but I had a feeling the bee tree was close.

The beeline seemed to continue across the field, down the hill, and into the tree line down near the creek. Tracking the bees through the woods was going to be a little tougher than it had been in the open. We proceeded down to the wooded creek bottom, found the best open area we could, and set up again. Once again I fired up the lamp and dripped on the honey, and once again the bees came in to the bait.

The first few bees that lifted off the bait circled and we lost them in the trees. However, the third one darted off through the trees in such a way that we were able to get a marginal fix on the course that she took. It seemed to be a continuation of the line we were following and my son, Kevin, took off in hot pursuit. Following a bee on foot through the woods is a pretty uneven contest. Therefore, I had little confidence that Kevin could keep up with the bee. My daughter and I continued to work the lantern and see if we couldn't bring in more bees. In thick woods such as these, with many small bushy trees, it is often necessary to get plenty of bees working the bait if a beeline is to be established.

In about ten minutes Kevin returned.

"I've got some good news and some bad news," he reported.

"Oh?"

"The bad news is that I lost sight of the bee."

"I figured you would. It's pretty thick in here."

"Wanna hear the good news?"

"Yep."

"I found the bee tree!"

And sure enough he had. Not 100 feet from where we had set up the bait was an old gray birch growing half in the creek and half out, and the bees were tumbling in and out of a split a few feet from the bottom of the tree. In less than forty-five minutes, *The Case of the Noisy Garbage Can* was solved and tree number 2 in Table 5.1 had been found. Sound easy doesn't it? It was that time. But it isn't always.

A CASE OF DOUBLE JEOPARDY—PART ONE

As pointed out in the last chapter, parks and the lawns of public buldings make good starting points if those lawns have white clover, dandelion, or some other flower that is receiving honey bee attention. Not far from my house is a grade school. Its baseball field contains quite a bit of white clover; both honey bees and bumblebees work the clover quite heavily. It occurred to me one day, as I was contemplating the peeling paint on the trim of my house, that the baseball field offered an excellent opportunity to take on another bee-sleuthing case. Besides, the alternative was to scrape and paint the house. It really wasn't much of a choice.

This time I had my bait box, and since the bees were already working the clover, there was no need to bring them in with a scent. Furthermore, since the bees were working white clover, it was a simple matter to plunk the vertical bait box over them and capture them. Plunk, plunk, plunk and in nothing flat I had twenty bees. I darkened the box, allowed the bees to load up, and then released them. From the initial release I got a line on two bees heading for a woodline to the north. The two took slightly different routes though and I wanted to get a better line and to time the bees. Therefore, I left the bait box in place, let the bees return to it, and set up a course.

Within half an hour, the bait box was just covered with bees, and I was continually having to squirt in more sugar water to keep the supply from being exhausted. Gradually I became more and more confident of the line to the north as one bee after another took off in that direction. Some went a little right and some a little left, but the centerline of the course was pretty clear. Yet one thing bothered me. I lost sight of about every third or fourth bee that lifted off the bait and circled even though the field was wide open and I was spotting the bees against a clear sky. I shifted position several times to get a better

In Double Jeopardy—Part One, a second beeline was established from the outfield of the ball field in order to get a better fix on the bee tree by intersection.

view of what was happening, and then I saw it. One bee lifted off the bait and started circling. But her circles drifted to the west, and then off she went like a shot straight west! It appeared that I had bees from two different colonies working the bait. Double jeopardy. Further observations confirmed this hypothesis. About one bee in three or four took off to the west. Were there any other clues? I examined the bees working the bait and, sure enough, some were definitely more yellow than the others. Fancy hybrid Italians? Maybe just some mongrel wild mix. But some of those bees sure were more yellow than the others. By watching the yellow bees as they took off, I was able to determine that they were the ones going west.

　　　　Which line to follow? The yellow bees were probably one of the hybrid commercial varieties and would certainly make a fine prize. I thought they would just look terrific working out of one of the hives in my back yard. On the other hand, there were more of the dark bees in the area, their course was much stronger, and their tree was probably closer. There is only one thing to do in such a situation. I pulled a five-cent executive decision maker out of my pocket: Heads I go west and tails I go north. Tails it was.

At this point I was again confronted with the problem described in the last case. The beeline that I was following soon disappeared into some heavy woods and the tracking in those woods would be difficult. Therefore I felt that I should be armed with all possible clues before proceeding. First I put a spot of blue chalk on a bee and timed her. She made three round trips in twenty-five minutes, from which I estimated the tree to be between ½ and ¾ of a mile away. Were there any other clues I could develop? How about intersection? It was worth a try.

I had been working near the infield of the ball field, so I moved out into deep center field, which was about as far as I could go without hitting more trees. I set up there, established another beeline to the tree to the north and estimated the point of intersection with the first beeline. As is so often the case with bee-sleuthing, the clue developed by intersection didn't agree exactly with the clue developed by timing the bee. The point of intersection appeared to be only ¼ to ½ mile down the original beeline, as opposed to the ½ to ¾ of a mile that I got by timing the bee. Although I didn't know it at the time, my second beeline was a little off and hence I did not have the point of intersection determined very accurately. As it later turned out, the timing method had given a very accurate estimate of the distance to the tree which was discovered to be ⅝ of a mile down the first beeline. But of course I had no way of knowing that—until I found the tree.

One thing I did not want to do was to go past the tree in the heavy forest cover. If I did, I could have trouble getting the bees started on the new bait location. Therefore, I decided to go only about ⅜ of a mile down the original beeline and then reset the bait box.

To this end I waited until the bait box was full of bees, sealed it up, and headed into the woods. Following a straight course through thick woods over uneven ground takes some degree of attention, but it can be done by judiciously selecting landmarks ahead. Once I had gone what I estimated to be about ⅜ of a mile, I started searching for a clearing. There was none to be had. The best I could come up with was a semiopen spot about ten yards across that was bordered on all sides by tall trees. I hung the bait box on a sapling in the middle of the opening and released the bees. As the bees came out of the box, they started circling. The more they circled, the higher they went. Up, up, and out through the little patch of sky that was visible through the trees straight overhead. By the time they got that high, there was no telling where they went. And I wasn't really too interested in where

Half an hour after the bees started working the bait in the soccer field, the box was covered with bees!

these first few bees went because when bees are moved in a bee box they get disoriented, and their initial beelines are not very reliable indicators of the true direction to the tree. What the bee hunter really wants is to get a good strong beeline established with a lot of bees working it. And I didn't want to do much scenting at this location for fear of bringing in bees from some other tree and getting really confused. I kept my bait boxes lightly scented with oil of anise, and I trusted that the scent plus the bees' innate sense of direction would enable them to find their way back.

After about fifteen minutes, a bee returned to the box. But when she left I lost her. A few minutes later another came back and I lost her also. It became clear that I was going to need a lot of bees working the bait, and that they were going to have to be familiar with the bait location so that they would not circle around so much when leaving the bait. So I filled up the honey comb with lots of sugar water and left with the idea of coming back later when there were more bees working the bait.

I returned a few hours later and there were seven or eight bees on the bait. I watched them for an hour or so, and every now and then saw one slip off the ridge to the north with very little circling. At least they seemed to be going north. If this was true, then I still hadn't passed the tree.

I left the bait box at that location for about a week, filling it up and checking it once or twice a day. Several times I thought I saw bees leave the bait and head north and my confidence began to build that I should relocate further north along the beeline, and that's just what I did. One day when about ten bees were in the box, I sealed it up and moved to the north about three hundred yards. This move took me off the ridgeline and down into a draw with a crack in it. And there my frustration began.

There weren't even any minor openings in the forest in this area, so I just picked an old dead pine and hung the box on the side of it. Getting the bees to work the bait was a snap and sometimes I would have twenty or thirty in the box, and a like number circling it on their way in or out. But seeing where they left the bait was nearly impossible. They would lift off and circle and immediately get lost in the trees. I left the bait in this location for a week, filling it, watching, and waiting. Finally by watching bees coming in, more so than those departing, I determined a beeline a little east of north. But I wasn't awfully confident of it. Yet it seemed right, and I knew I was close to the tree so I started looking. I checked every tree over eighteen inches in diameter in that general direction between my bait and the point where the woods opened up onto a soccer field. Nothing. I widened the area of my search. I started checking trees as small as twelve inches. Nothing. By the time I stopping checking trees, I felt like I was checking broomsticks. Still nothing. Where could they be going? I had timed some bees and knew that I was within a quarter of a mile of the tree. The bee-sleuth was obviously in need of more clues, but how was he to get them? Then it struck me. The soccer field! It was only a quarter of a mile away and it was the perfect place to establish another beeline so that I could find the bee by intersection.

And that's just what I did. After receiving that little brainstorm, the rest was easy. I emptied my bait box of all bees and went to the soccer field where I captured some bees that were working in clover. Since I knew I was close to the tree, I felt fairly confident that at least some of the bees in the soccer field would be from the tree for which I was looking. Soon I had a good strong course of bees working from the bait, and in the wide-open space of the soccer field, it was easy to get a line on them. Sure enough, this new line indicated that I should have been looking further west than I had been. I took off on the new beeline and half an hour later I found my tree. A stream of dark honey bees was pouring in and out of a big hollow walnut tree (tree number 3 in Table 5.1). I was still somewhat puzzled, though, over why my previous beeline from the dead pine had taken me too far

When the tree was finally spotted in Double Jeopardy—Part One, it was nearly overlooked. Several obvious openings on one side of the tree contained no bees. The opening the bees were using was on the far side.

to the east. Now that I knew where the bee tree was, I went back to the pine tree to investigate. I set up my bait box and soon had a good number of bees working the bait. I walked down the apparent beeline to the northeast keeping the location of the tree in mind. Then, as I started to cross the creek that the bee tree was on, I realized what the bees were doing. They were flying northeast, which was the shortest distance to the creek, and then turning left and flying up the creek bed. The creek was a pretty good-sized one, so the air space immediately above it was clear and the bees were using it like a pipeline to and from the tree. Sometimes one gets a crooked beeline like that. But that's what makes it interesting.

In spite of a deceiving clue in the form of a crooked beeline, I had managed to find the tree, and finding the tree is the real triumph for the bee hunter. It really doesn't matter whether or not he can cut the tree down. I wouldn't in my wildest dreams have cut down that twisted old walnut. It doesn't really even matter if you can get the bees and the honey without cutting down the tree. The satisfaction is tracking the bee to his lair and knowing that not one person in ten thousand can do it. That's the real prize.

A CASE OF DOUBLE JEOPARDY—PART TWO

Now that the first part of the case was solved, there remained a question of international intrigue; namely, where was the base of operations of the Italians? Recall that when we started out hunt in the school yard we had two beelines, one of which was a course of yellow Italian bees that went west. The course was not very strong, but I was sure it was strong enough that it could be followed.

One problem with following the course to the west was that

Once the beeline is established, it is necessary to periodically refill the comb with sugar water; the bees can empty it surprisingly quickly.

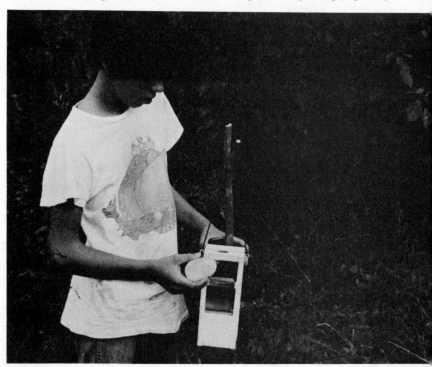

the area west of the school was quite developed and it was going to be hard to find places to set up my bait boxes without intruding on private property and tramping through backyards. In addition, the tree the bees were in could well be a big shade tree in the middle of someone's lawn and I wouldn't even be able to get close enough to inspect it. I could see that this was going to be a challenge.

From my previous hunt, I knew the approximate direction of the beeline. I followed this line to the western-most extremity of the school property, which was where the private land begins. Here I used my vertical bait box and captured a group of bees working in white clover in an effort to establish a more accurate beeline. Soon I had bees from both colonies working the bait, but this time the percentage of Italian bees on the bait was higher, since I had moved two or three hundred yards closer to their colony and away from the other colony. The westward beeline went across a street to the west and over two houses which were surrounded by large trees. If the bees were in one of those trees, I was in trouble. But beyond the houses and about a quarter of a mile away was an empty lot where I could set up again. So I waited until there were about a dozen bees in the box, sealed it up, and headed for the lot.

I selected a spot in the middle of the lot free of any nearby trees and released the bees. About half of them flew into the air circling confusedly and then took off. A few went northeast, obviously headed toward the tree I had found previously. But several continued on to the west.

The other half of the bees sat around in their usual exasperating manner, rubbing their legs and primping themselves. They often do this after working a piece of honey comb that is really covered with sugar water, and I presume it's because they get the sticky mess all over themselves. But one by one they eventually took off, some going northeast and some continuing on to the west.

West of the vacant lot was a five to ten acre wooded tract, beyond which were more houses. I hoped that the bees were in the woodlot since I knew who owned it and I felt that I could get permission to cut the tree down.

But I needed more information. I could spend a lot of time searching through the trees in that lot since it contained numerous big trees. And if it turned out that the tree was really half a mile beyond the lot, the time spent looking for the tree in the woodlot would all be wasted. Some bee hunters would have done just that; they would have jumped right in and started checking trees. But for me, part of the fun in bee hunting comes from trying to deduce as

In Double Jeopardy—Part Two, the bee hole was located about 25 feet above the ground in an oak tree.

accurately as possible the exact location of the tree. Why use brute force and ignorance when skill and daring are available?

To determine whether or not the tree was likely to be in the woodlot, I needed to determine the approximate distance to the tree. This meant that I had to mark and time a bee which, in turn, meant that the bees had to start working my bait. So I waited for one to return. And I waited. And I waited. After an hour, none had returned to the bait box, and if they don't come back in an hour they aren't going to. Sometimes that happens, although I don't know why. The bait box was painted white and was scented with anise oil and was sitting in plain sight in the middle of the lot. But no bees.

Twice I returned to the school yard and captured more bees and twice the same results. These Italians were smarter than I had given them credit for being. Either that, or they were too dumb to find their way back. I suspected that the bees were being diverted by some other particularly rich pasture and just weren't coming back to the bait box. Finally, after the third trip back to the school to reload with bees—success! I had released the bees and was waiting for them to return when I heard something buzz over my head. A bee? My heart beat a little faster. The next thing I knew, there she was hovering over the bait like a gold and silver helicopter. Lower, lower, touchdown! I knew that I'd have my beeline in just a few minutes now.

Once the bees set up the beeline, the rest was easy. They started to work the bait heavily, and I was able to determine more accurately the direction to the tree. I was also able to mark a bee and to time her round trip as about four and one half minutes, so I knew I was close—probably a quarter of a mile or less. I took off down the beeline and within fifteen minutes found the tree. (I walked by it once because I was too lazy to walk around and check the far side.) The tree was a tall oak and the bees had found themselves an opening into the trunk about twenty-five feet off the ground. Part Two of the Case of Double Jeopardy had been solved, and tree number 6 in Table 5.1 had been located.

OTHER COMMENTS

Old-time bee hunters used to practice their craft, and in some cases still do, in the rural and mountainous farm country and forests of Appalachia, the Ozarks, the Pacific Northwest, and other lightly populated areas of the country. But as the preceding examples show, honey bees are everywhere. And bee trees are rather like lunker bass and trophy deer in that they're where you find them. The big difference, though, between the bees and the deer and bass is that you won't find the latter in the middle of town. The former you may.

It's been a long time since I've been in Central Park in New York City. But one of these days I'll get back there, and when I do I intend to take along a few pieces of bee hunting gear. I'll bet that there are bee trees to be found in the heart of Gotham.

7. Cutting the Tree

The Honey is sweet, but the Bee has a sting.
> BENJAMIN FRANKLIN c. 1732
> *Poor Richard's Almanac*

Ouch!
Ouch!
Ouch!

> KEVIN DONOVAN, NOVEMBER 1978
> PERSONAL COMMUNICATION, WHILE
> CUTTING DOWN A BEE TREE.

The things which hurt, instruct.

> BENJAMIN FRANKLIN c. 1732
> *Poor Richard's Almanac*

Once you have located a colony of wild honey bees, you will probably want to capture the bees and extract the honey. The most common place to find wild bees is in an old hollow tree; and the most common methods of capturing the bees and removing the honey require that the tree be cut down. Sometimes, however, the bees will be found in rock formations, in the walls of houses, or in trees that can't be cut down. Removal of the bees and honey in such cases is treated in the next chapter. This chapter deals with those techniques that involve cutting down the tree.

INITIAL CONSIDERATIONS

One caution should be expressed before describing the bee tree cutting and bee capturing methods. In many instances the bee hunters will find the bees in an old tree that he is free to cut down or which he can easily obtain permission to cut down. Such trees are often of little or no lumber value and appear to have no redeeming social importance. But before laying an ax to the tree or cranking up the chainsaw, look around. Are you in a mature forest where there are plenty of other large old trees (often called "wolf trees"), or has the area recently been cut over leaving few big trees as potential den trees for birds, animals, and bees? The processes that create big hollow trees are very slow compared to the workings of the chain saw. If there are few potential den trees in the area, it is better that the tree be left standing and that the bee hunter use one of the nondestructive methods described in the next chapter to get his bees and honey. Or he can simply mark the tree and take his satisfaction from having successfully located it.

If, however, there are lots of potential den trees in the area, cutting down the bee tree will do no harm and in addition to bees and honey the tree may also provide a few loads of firewood. Or to state it more accurately, cutting down the tree will do no harm provided you have permission to cut it down. In the *ABC and XYZ of Bee Culture*, first published in 1877, A.I. Root and E.R. Root offered this advice concerning the cutting down of bee trees:

NEVER QUARREL ABOUT BEE-TREES

When you have found your tree, go at once to the owner of the land, and get permission to take your bees. No matter what the law allows, do nothing in his absence you would not do if he were standing by, and do your work with as clear a conscience as you would work in your own bee-yard. Many quarrels and disagreements and much hard feeling have been engendered by cutting bee-trees. If I am correctly informed, bees are the property of whoever finds them first; and on this account it is customary to cut the initials of the finder, with the date, in the body of the tree; but you have no more right to cut the owner's timbers without permission than you have to cut his corn. I have never found any one inclined to withhold consent, when he was politely asked for permission to get our bees out of the trees. I do not wonder that people feel cross when their timber is mutilated by roving idlers, and I can scarcely blame them for giving a wholesome lesson now and then just then to remind us that we have laws in our country for their protection. I hope my readers will have no disposition to trespass on the premises or rights of any one, without permission. The most difficult and particular person in your neighborhood will, in all probability, be found pleasant and accommodating, if you go to him in a pleasant and neighborly way.

More than 100 years later, that is still pretty good advice.

There are two general methods of cutting a bee tree. One method consists of cutting the hollow portion of the tree into short sections (gums) for transport back home, while the other method consists of splitting or wedging the tree in place and removing the

Examining the bees' entrance hole beforehand will give some idea of the size of the colony and some hint of where to make the cuts.

honey and bees at the site of the tree. With either technique, it is possible to insure survival of the colony, and the bee hunter should give careful consideration to how he proceeds to insure that the colony is not destroyed. The tree can be cut down virtually any time of year and the colony will survive if the bee hunter gives adequate consideration to the needs of the bees. If, for example, the tree is cut down in late fall or winter, and if all the honey is taken at that time, the colony will surely starve to death before spring comes. This unhappy turn of events can be avoided if the bee hunter takes the precautions described below. To allow the colony to starve to death is not only wasteful of wildlife, but also is short-sighted when it comes to next year's honey supply.

FELLING THE TREE

Whether the tree is to be split in place or cut up into gums, the first step is to cut the tree down. Before starting to cut, try to puff some smoke into the colony. This will tend to keep the bees calm and will help prevent them from swarming into the air. If the configuration of the tree is such that the bees cannot be smoked beforehand, the smoke should be ready as soon as the tree hits the ground. The more bees that get into the air, the longer the collection process will take and the greater the chances of getting stung. The bees can be smoked with one of the smokers described in Chapter 3, or an oily rag can be ignited and held in the hollow of the tree. If the rag continues to smolder, it can be left in the tree to continue smoking while the cutting is in progress. Just be sure to keep your fire under control, and don't smoke the bees so heavily that you drive them out of the tree.

Old-timers took great pride in not wearing any protective clothing while "robbin' the bee." I don't recommend such a cavalier approach. Many of these old-timers had been stung so many times that they developed an immunity to bee venom. It has been estimated that it takes about fifty stings per year to develop and maintain such an immunity. I manage to get thirty or forty stings per year and I can assure you that each one still hurts; so I cover up.

The most important item of protective gear is a mask of some type to cover the head and face. Stings around the eyes and ears can be painful and occasionally dangerous, so whatever you wear be sure that your head covering is sealed around the neck in such a way that the bees can't get up inside it. Nothing is more disconcerting than having an angry bee buzzing around inside your face mask that couldn't get away if she wanted to.

Similarly, gloves should be sealed at the wrists and pants bottoms should be tucked into boots, or tied off, or sealed with rubber bands to keep the bees out. (Just as one does not want an angry bee trapped in his face mask, one does not want an angry bee trapped in his britches. Some of the stings that could result from a bee in your knickers are too painful to even contemplate.) Usually, one layer of clothing is sufficient to protect against stings. However, if you are particularly concerned about being stung, double up. I have been stung through denim jeans and gloves often enough to know that one layer of clothing doesn't *always* suffice. If in spite of everything you get stung, the hints in Chapter 2 will help somewhat. But not much.

When cutting down a big old tree in the woods, be careful. Such trees have a way of getting hung up on other trees and of not falling exactly where you expected. Try to drop the tree in the direction that will cause the least shock and vibration to the colony inside. The impact of the tree hitting the ground will often break up some of the comb, excite the bees, and may cause honey to run all over the place. The impact can be reduced by dropping the tree uphill rather than down so it doesn't have so far to fall. Other trees can be used to cushion the fall. If the bee tree has a good growth of branches on one

When cutting down the
tree, avoid hitting
the colony with the saw,
and try to drop the
tree as gently as
possible to prevent
unnecessary damage to
the combs of brood
and honey.

side, it may be possible to drop the tree in such a way that the branches help cushion the fall. In any event, "the easier the fall, the easier the robbin'."

If the bees have been smoked, they will often remain surprisingly calm during the tree cutting process, provided that the tree is cut with a saw. The repeated thumps of an ax, however, will usually get them excited no matter how much advance preparation is done. It is sometimes possible to keep the bees in the tree by simply plugging up their entrances. This works well except during periods when the bees are out working in the field. At such times the worker bees, as they return from the field, will find their entrance into the tree blocked and they will start circling the tree excitedly. You will quickly come to the conclusion that you would have been better off if you let them in. On the other hand, if you are cutting the tree during the fall or winter when few bees are out, sealing the tree will at least keep the bees inside during the cutting operation. Don't be fooled into thinking that just because it's fall or even the dead of winter that the bees won't come out to defend their homes. Even in the coldest weather, bees in the center of the winter cluster (see Chapter 2) are warm and active, and these workers will be released from the hive like guided missiles to drive off the intruder. If the temperature is very cold, these bees probably won't last more than a few minutes before dying in the snow. But in nature's scheme of things, the loss of a few hundred bees is a small price to pay for saving the colony.

One way to seal the tree with the bees inside during warm weather is to pay a visit to the bee tree the night before it is to be cut.

The tree can then be sealed with the entire worker force inside. Don't make your seal airtight or you will run the risk of suffocating the colony. Fly screen makes a good sealing material.

CUTTING THE TREE INTO GUMS

Once the tree is cut down, the honey removal and bee capture effort can begin. The tree can either be split (also called wedging) or it can be cut up into short sections called gums. The gums containing the bees and the honey are then transported home for further processing. The advantages of cutting the tree into gums are:

- Virtually every bee and every scrap of honey and comb are recovered.
- If the bee hunter wants to keep some bees in gums at home, this method will get him some gums.
- If the gums are not to be used to keep bees, they can be split up for firewood.
- If the cutting is done during very cold weather, this is the only practical way to assure survival of the colony. The splitting method described in the next section results in too much exposure of the bees.

The disadvantages of cutting the tree into gums are:

- The gums can be heavy, and if the tree is in a remote area it may be impractical to carry the gums out.
- The tree is destroyed and can no longer be used by bees.
- There is one colony of bees before the cutting and only one colony afterwards, namely the one you take with you. In the tree splitting method, the colony is divided with viable colony left in the woods and one taken home.

Once you have weighed the pros and cons, if you decide you want to cut the tree into gums, here's how to do it.

First, determine the extent of the colony and how much of the tree is filled with comb. It is desirable to make as few cuts as possible through the comb. Cutting through the comb will spill a lot of honey, kill brood, and if you are unlucky, may even kill the queen. Often, the bottom or top of the cavity will be full of darkened unused comb. This comb can be cut through without doing any damage. The extent of the cavity can usually be estimated fairly accurately by looking up the bottom of the fallen tree, checking through holes and splits in the tree, and by tapping on the tree to determine the extent of the hollow cavity.

Once the tree is on the ground, determine where the cuts will be made to divide it into gums. The tin cans in this picture mark the cuts that will be made above and below the colony. The two rocks mark cuts that will be made through the colony. These latter cuts will do some damage but probably not too much. The cuts shown here will produce three gums.

Once the extent of the colony is determined, decide where you will make the crosscuts to cut the tree into gums. The gums must not be so long that they will be too heavy for you, and any assistants that you may have, to carry the gums out of the woods. I have rolled gums out, but if the combs inside are weak or too heavy with honey they will break up and create a mess. If the gums are later to be used for keeping bees, sections two to three feet long should do nicely. And of course, in selecting the places where you want to cut, try to minimize cutting through filled comb. If the hollow section is short enough, you may be able to cut through the solid wood above and below the colony. This will keep the bees from coming out through the ends of the gum after those cuts are made. If, in addition, you sealed the openings into the gum the night before, you will have a completely captive colony.

I recall the first bee tree I ever cut. The tree was a dead pine. My son had spotted the bees flying in and out one day while we were out hiking. The following fall we went back to collect the honey and firewood. I was somewhat uneducated at the time and had no intention of preserving my bees. So the first good cold fall day that came along, off we went with chainsaws and protective clothing to "take up th' bee."

In nothing flat, I was up to my ears in bees, honey, and sawdust. I had honey in my chainsaw, on my gloves, and in my hair. The bees were a little slow because of the temperature (about 45°F), but still a good many of them managed to get into the air. Soon we had five sections of bee gum, all of which showed some promise of containing honey, which we loaded into a wheelbarrow and headed for the car. Since I had no intention of keeping any bees, I simply loaded the gums into an open utility trailer and started home. When we arrived home half an hour later, I was surprised to find that the bees had not flown or been blown away. Rather, most of them had congregated in one section of gum. Although I didn't realize it at the time, this was undoubtedly the section with the queens in it. The other four sections of gum I split up and extracted the comb and honey. But somehow it just didn't seem right to split that section with all the bees in it, and to thereby sentence the entire colony to death by starvation.

Once the cut locations have been determined, simply slice the tree up into a number of short sections or gums.

When the tree is cut into gums, these cuts made through the
colony will expose combs and may release honey. The bees will tend to
mass on any broken comb.

So I took that one section of gum, set it upright on a piece of plywood
on some cinder blocks, and put a board over it to keep the rain out.

I didn't give that bee gum much thought through the balance
of the winter, and I had no idea whether the bees were surviving or
not. But then, when the first warm day of spring came, there they
were! Worker bees were flying out of the gum to collect pollen and
nectar for the colony. They made it!

Since those early days, I have gotten a lot smarter about
cutting a tree into sections. First of all, once the sections have been
cut, give the bees about half an hour to settle back down. This pause
will give most of the bees time to fly back into óne of the gums,
thereby reducing losses. Second, take along some screen wire and
tacks or a staple gun and fasten a piece of screen wire over both ends
of gum. This will keep the bees in the gums while they are being
transported. Third, protect the gums while they are being transported, especially if the weather is cold. If the gums are thrown into an
open trailer and transported at forty or fifty miles per hour in such a

Carrying the gums is hard work. While tracking the bee, pray that
you'll find it in a pine and not an oak since the pine is much lighter. And
when you do find the tree, don't cut the pieces too big or you'll
have trouble carrying them.

way that the cold winter air is allowed to rush through the gums, the
bees will freeze to death. Finally, upon arrival home, set the section
with the queen upright and elevated slightly off the ground. Then as
the other sections of gum are split, the bees on the comb from those
gums can be brushed into the gum with the queen in it. For more
details on this transfer operation, see Chapter 9. If the weather is
warm enough for the bees to fly, it is often possible to simply set up
the queen gum, set the other gums nearby, and let the bees relocate
themselves. They will naturally congregate in the section that contains the queen.

From the foregoing discussion, do not conclude that cutting
the tree into gums is appropriate only during cold weather. This
method can be used year round and the only major difference between
summer and winter cutting is that the amount of honey left with the
bees to insure their survival will vary depending on the time of year.
From the time that the honey flow begins in the spring until midsummer, it is possible to remove most of the honey from the colony

Before moving the gums any great distance, staple screen wire over the end if you plan to keep the bees, as this will help keep them in the gums during transportation. Note the number of excited bees flying around during this operation.

and the bees will still have enough time to store more before the winter comes. But from late summer on, the needs of the bees must be considered. A wintering colony needs from twenty pounds of honey (in the South) to forty pounds of honey (northern tier states) to make it through the winter. Don't be guilty of squeezing the last few drops of honey out of the colony and thereby subjecting it to death by starvation. Occasionally a tree will be cut down that contains no honey, or that contains so little honey that there is none that the bee hunter can take in good conscience. That's life. On the other hand, I have heard of rare cases of tree trees containing 200 to 300 pounds of honey, and once heard of an old abandoned farmhouse chimney which yielded over 350 pounds of honey.

Up to this point, this chapter has discussed cutting the tree as though the bee hunter were going to keep the bees and take them

If the bee hunter doesn't care to take the bees home and keep them, they can be left in a section of gum in the woods. Stand the gum on end, nail a few boards over the top, and make sure the bees have a way in and out.

home. For me, capturing the bees and bringing them home to keep is one of the most satisfying parts of the sport of bee hunting. But keeping bees isn't for everyone. Some people won't be interested in keeping bees and others, by their circumstances, are effectively prevented from doing so. If either situation applies to you, you can still extract the honey from the tree by cutting the tree into gums. Only instead of setting up the gum containing the queen in your backyard or apiary, set it up in the woods right where you cut down the tree. Split the other gums right there, transfer the bees to the queen gum and leave with just your honey, and the firewood if you want it.

Usually the section of gum containing the queen will also contain most of the brood comb (comb containing developing bee larvae). If in splitting the other sections of gum you come across any substantial amount of brood comb, separate it out from the honey

comb and try to insert it back into the queen gum. By so doing you will
be giving the brood a chance to develop and emerge, thereby strength-
ening the colony.

SPLITTING THE TREES

The second method of removing the bees and honey consists of splitting the tree. If the tree is split, a fallen but otherwise intact tree is
left behind, and enough bees are left in the tree so that they can
establish a viable colony. Splitting the tree is a particularly useful
technique in remote areas since it involves carrying a minimum of
equipment into and out of the woods.

When splitting the tree, the trunk or the branch containing
the bees is usually not literally split into two pieces. Rather, a rectangular slab is split out of the side of the trunk thereby allowing access
to the bees and the honey inside. The slab that is cut out is typically
twelve to eighteen inches wide and three to six feet long, depending
on the diameter of the tree and the length of the section of the tree
containing honey.

If the tree is to be split, smoke the bees before cutting the tree
down and then do it again as soon as the tree hits the ground. This
will help keep the bees from taking to the air. As was the case when
the tree was being sawed up into gums, an effort must be made to
determine the extent of the colony. As described above, this is done by
looking in the end of the trunk, examining any openings or holes in
the trunk, and by tapping on the trunk to determine the extent of the
hollow cavity. Once the extent of the colony has been estimated,
proceed as follows.

At one end of the colony, start to cut through the trunk as
though you were going to make a perpendicular cut across the grain
right through the trunk and cut it in two. However, you should stop
this cut when it is about one third of the way through the tree. Make
sure that this cut is deep enough that your saw blade penetrates into
the hollow portion of the tree. Once this cut is completed, move to the
other end of the colony and make a similar cut. These two cuts, once
completed, will establish the ends of the slab that is to be removed
from the trunk.

The next step is to connect the end cuts with longer cuts
running lengthwise down the trunk. These longer cuts will form the
sides of the slab that is to be removed. There is an important difference between the end cuts and side cuts that should be noted at
this point. The end cuts are made at either extremity of the colony,

As soon as the tree hits the ground, puff some smoke into
any openings that connect with the cavity where the colony is.
This will help keep the bees calm.

and hence there is nothing wrong with allowing the tip of the saw to
penetrate into the hollow cavity in the trunk. However, in making
the cuts lengthwise down the trunk, you will be making two cuts right
past the heart of the colony and right past the mass of bees and honey
comb. When making these cuts, every effort must be made to keep the
saw blade out of the trunk cavity. If a chainsaw blade were run down
the trunk twice (once for each of the side cuts) and were allowed to
penetrate all the way into the cavity each time, many bees would be
killed, much of the brood would be lost, and the honey comb would be
churned into a gooey, runny mess full of sawdust and splinters. Therefore, when making the side cuts, it is better to err on the side of
making these cuts a little too shallow rather than making them too
deep.

When splitting a slab out of the side of the trunk, begin with two cuts across the grain, one at either end of the intended slab These cuts must go clear through to the cavity inside the log.

The two cuts across the grain are connected by two cuts down the length of the trunk. These latter cuts form the sides of the slab. When making these cuts down the trunk, be sure your saw does not penetrate the hollow portion of the tree, thereby destroying the comb inside.

Once the side cuts are made, the slab should theoretically fall or lift right off the trunk, but due to misalignment of the cuts and irregularity of the body cavity, it never does. It is at this point that the ax and log splitting edges are broken out. By placing two wedges into one of the side cuts, and then hammering them in with the back of the ax, the slab can usually be split out without much difficulty.

If the bees have been relatively peaceful up to this point, you can expect that they will become excited as soon as you start hammering on the wedges. The thumping on the side of the trunk will bring them tumbling out through the saw cuts like so many fighter pilots to defend the colony. So before doing any wedging or hammering on the trunk, be sure you are covered up.

This discussion so far has been couched in terms of doing all cutting operations with a chainsaw. Using a chainsaw is the quickest and easiest way to go. However, if you do not have a chainsaw at your disposal or are not inclined to use one, the entire job can be done with hand tools. An ax and a few wedges are all that is required. The end cuts for slabs can be formed by cutting V-shaped notches part way

Once the cuts outlining the slab have been completed,
the slab can be loosened up with wedges and the back of an ax.

Pull the slab away
carefully to ensure that
no more damage
than necessary is done
to the comb inside.

through the trunk, and the side cuts would simply be long splits made with the axes and wedges. It is this process that gives rise to the term "wedging the tree."

Once the slab is removed, lay it aside since you will need it again later. You are now ready to start removing bees and comb from the tree. And now the fun begins.

I am sometimes amazed at just how much disturbance bees will tolerate without attacking. If you keep them at home in domestic hives, you can take off the cover and lift out frames of honey and they won't bother you. In the woods, you can set a ladder up against their tree and peer in or take pictures and they will ignore you. You can cut down their tree and often cause little more than minor excitement. The wedging operations will probably put a lot of bees into the air, but they may or may not be very aggressive.

But all that changes when you reach for their comb! As sections of brood and honeycomb are torn from the trees, the bees are transformed into ferocious and aggressive little dynamos, and the ferocity of their attack can be absolutely intimidating in spite of all your protective clothing. When you reach in and grab a piece of comb and start to tear it from the tree, the bees will fly into a rage and bombard your hand. You will feel the impact of their bodies right through your glove. If you withdraw your hand and examine it, you will find anywhere from a few to fifteen or twenty furious bees firmly grasping your glove, and they will be beating their wings and arching their backs just looking for a way to get their stingers into you. Their wings will be whirring so violently that you will feel the vibrations through your gloves and it will make your whole hand tingle. (Your hand may also be trembling a little, but that's a different matter.)

Since such an attack by the bees is a somewhat unnerving experience, it is fortunate for the bee hunter that this period of extreme aggressiveness lasts for only ten or fifteen minutes. For some reason, the bees start to calm down again after that. Perhaps they become exhausted by the intensity of their excitement. Maybe they get disorganized and disoriented as the colony is torn apart. But whatever the reason, they invariably calm down after a while, even if the comb removal is still going on.

The comb will usually tear out of the tree in large flat slabs. If the bees are to be kept, one or two large pieces of comb containing brood should be placed in the bee transport box (see Chapter 3 for

After the slab is removed, the comb can be worked loose from the tree. Separate the sheets of brood comb from the honey comb. The brood comb will be returned to the tree.

(Left) Several pieces of comb should be placed in the transport box. Bees from the remaining pieces of comb can then be brushed into the box.

(Right) Once the brood comb has been returned to the tree, the slab must be put back in place. Slabs cut out of the tops of trees can just be rested in place; those cut from the sides of fallen trees must be nailed or tied back.

construction details). These slabs will have bees plastered on both sides of the slab. By placing these pieces of comb in the box, you will have captured several hundred to several thousand bees, and the comb in the box will give subsequent bees something to cling to, thereby making them less likely to fly from the box while the lid is open and you are working. As each subsequent piece of comb is removed, the bees should be brushed off the comb and into the box. Some will fly out, but most will stay, especially if the queen is in the box. It is often difficult to locate the queen in the confusion of the comb removal operation, but you should be alert for any large groups or knots of bees. The other bees may try to congregate around the queen, and if any large group of bees is spotted, the whole bunch should be brushed into the box. Capturing the queen is not absolutely essential, but it makes the collection process easier and it will get your colony off to a good start when you get the bees home. How to determine for sure whether or not you have the queen, and what to do about it if you didn't get her, are described in Chapter 9.

As the comb is removed from the tree, it should be sorted into comb that is primarily brood and comb that is primarily honey. From the time the honey (nectar) starts to flow in the spring until midsummer, you can remove virtually all of the honey in the tree and the bees will have time to replenish it. From midsummer on, care must be taken to insure that the remaining bees have enough honey to see them through the coming winter.

Once the comb is removed and sorted and you have captured all the bees that you can get into your transport box, close up the transport box to keep any more bees from flying out. Then the reconstruction of the hive begins. Regardless of how many bees you managed to get into the box, there will still be thousands that are free. They will be swarming in the air, collecting on branches, and some will still be returning from the field unaware of what has happened to their home. These thousands of free bees will form the nucleus of the colony that is to remain in the tree. At this point it should be clear why the splitting method of capturing bees and removing honey is applicable only in fairly warm weather. There is so much exposure of the bees during the cutting and transfer operation that there would be a high risk of losing the colony if it were done in cold weather.

To reconstruct the hive, begin by placing the brood comb and any honeycomb that is to be returned to the bees back into the cavity of the tree so as to stand vertically. Begin by laying in a row of comb against one side of the trunk cavity. It is important that successive layers of comb not be placed right up against one another, since the bees work both sides of the comb and a bee space is needed between successive rows of comb. In reconstructing the hive, provide this bee space by inserting thin (¼″ to ½″) twigs into the cavity between the successive rows of comb. Note also that when bees build honeycomb cells, they do not make the cells horizontal. Instead, each cell in the comb angles slightly upward. Among other things, this slight upward orientation helps hold the thin watery honey in the cell while it is ripening. Since the tree has been cut down and is now lying on its side, all of the honey comb is also lying on its side. When placing the comb back in the tree, the orientation of the comb should be corected to insure that the axis of the comb that was vertical before the tree was cut is once again vertical. This should be done with all comb that is returned to the tree regardless of whether it contains brood or honey. It may be necessary to cut and fit the comb to achieve this reorientation.

When the slab is returned to the tree, cover any large cracks or openings with boards, stones, bark or other material to keep the rain out.
Don't forget to plug the hole, if there is one, at the bottom of the tree.
Just be sure to leave an opening somewhere for the bees to get in and out.

Once the comb has been reinserted into the tree, the next step is to replace the rectangular slab of trunk that was split out previously. If the slab was split out of the top of the trunk, it will be possible to simply rest the slab back into place. If the slab was cut from the side of the trunk, it will be necessary to tie or nail it back.

Even once the slab is returned to the trunk, it will not provide adequate protection for the bees inside. The cutting and wedging operations will leave many places where rainwater can run into the trunk. These places should be covered with boards, pieces of bark, stones, or other materials to keep the rain out of the colony. In addition, if there is a large opening at the base of the trunk where the tree was cut off, this opening should be blocked off to keep out predators (especially skunks and bears), rain, cold air, and light.

With these tasks completed, the bee hunter is ready to return home. The bees and brood comb in his transport box will form the nucleus of a new colony at home. The colony he has left in the woods will rebuild itself and if the bee hunter takes their queen, that colony will raise a new one, provided the bee hunter has been careful to leave some young brood. And the best part of leaving a viable colony in the woods is that next year the bee hunter can come back and again remove bees and honey from the same tree. Only the next time, the tree will already be cut down and split, and all the bee hunter will have to do is open it up and help himself.

8. Non-Destructive Capture Methods

"I think the bees suspect something."
"What sort of thing?"
"I don't know, but something tells me that they're
suspicious."
"Perhaps they think that you're after their honey."
"It may be that. You can never tell with bees."

CHRISTOPHER ROBIN AND
WINNIE-THE-POOH IN
The World of Pooh, BY
A.A. MILNE

Remove not the landmarks which thy fathers have set.
PROVERBS 22:28

If the bee hunter practices his craft in urban or surburban settings, he will frequently find that he has tracked his quarry to a tree that can't be cut down. It may be on public property, or it may be someone's favorite shade tree; but whatever the reason, it can't be destroyed. Sometimes the bees will be found in a tree that is so big it just isn't worth cutting. An oak that's three and a half feet in diameter puts a lot of wear and tear on a chainsaw, to say nothing of the wear and tear on the logger. And sometimes bees will be found in rock formations. Rock formations will also put a lot of wear and tear on the chainsaw.

Bees get into buildings fairly frequently, where they take up residence between the walls and under floors. In some cases a few boards can be pulled off to gain access to the bees, but more often than not they are found holed up in some space that would require too much damage to the building if access were to be gained.

In all of these cases, some non-destructive method of capturing the colony is needed. In the methods described below, not only are the bees captured and converted into a domesticated colony, but also the honey is retrieved. The methods described below are the only sure and humane ways that I know of to remove bees from some area

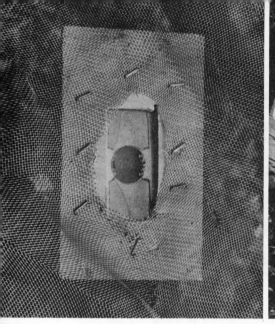

If the bee hole that is to be blocked off is large, the bee escape can be secured to a piece of plywood with a hole in it. The piece of plywood is stapled onto a piece of screen with a hole in it. Once the screen is stapled over the bees' entrance, the screen should be covered with dark cloth. After this is done, the only light the bees see will be coming from the escape, and they will move quickly in that direction.

where they are a nuisance, but where a tree or building must not be damaged. Some people advocate removal methods that involve killing the colony with any one of several poisonous gases or with smoke. In some of these methods the honey is subsequently removed from the tree and in some it is not. I have no use for any technique that calls for killing the bees with poisonous materials, and I will not describe the methods nor name the poisons here. My techniques involve saving the bees, the honey, and the tree or house.

REMOVAL FROM TREES

The most common capture problem confronting the bee hunter is the case of the tree that cannot be cut down. The basic plan of attack is simple. First, the hole or holes that the bees are using to get in and out of the tree are altered in such a way that the bees can get out, but then cannot get back in. Second, an alternate home is provided for them outside the tree. Third, you give them a queen in their new home. And fourth, once all the bees are happily housed in their new home outside the tree and are adjusted and acclimated to that home, you allow them to return to their old home in the tree to remove the honey. So much for the grand strategy, now for the details.

Begin by insuring that you have located all the openings that the bees are using and block all of them off but one. The openings can be blocked with some material such as screen wire, but be sure to further cover the opening with an opaque material such as dark cloth. The bees are drawn to the light when they try to exit the tree, and you don't want them congregating at these other blocked-off openings. If there are any other large openings in the tree that the bees are not using, these openings should also be blocked. Once the bees are locked out of the tree, you want them to take up residence in the hive that you provide for them, and not in some other hole in the tree.

Once all the other openings are blocked, you are ready to tackle the main opening. The device that allows the bees to get out of the tree but not back in is a clever little piece of beekeeping equipment called a bee escape. It is a small (about one inch by three inches) device with a hole in the center and several thin metal flappers that allow the bee to pass through the hole on her way out, but do not allow her reentry. It's an inexpensive item that can be obtained from any bee supply house. Get several.

Next cut yourself a small piece of board or plywood (about four inches by four inches) and cut an opening in the center of it to accommodate the bee escape. Nail or staple the bee escape in place. Then cut a piece of screen wire large enough to cover the opening in the bee tree, and when cutting it, leave six inches to a foot of surplus around the edges to insure that you have plenty of material to work with to seal off the hole. The next step is to install the piece of plywood with the bee escape in it into the center of the screen. To do this, cut a hole in the center of the screen and make the hole slightly smaller than the piece of plywood. Staple the plywood in place in the center of the screen.

If you have done all this, you now have a piece of screen wire large enough to cover the opening in the tree with a bee escape installed in the middle of the screen. The next step is obvious. Secure the screen over the opening in the tree. When you do so, make sure that you have the correct side of the bee escape facing outward. It doesn't do much good to orient the escape so that the bees can get into the tree but not out; that just traps the bees in the tree. And when you are securing the screen over the opening, use plenty of nails and staples to insure that the screen is tightly sealed all around the hole. If the bees find so much as one small cranny through which they can slip back into the tree, they will do so; if that happens, the whole sealing job will be ineffective. Look for wrinkles in the screen and irregularities in the bark of the tree through which the bees may be able to slip back inside.

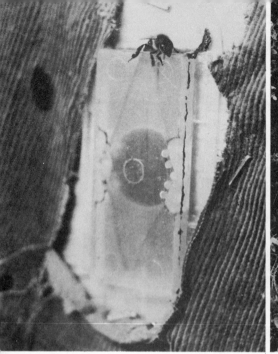

(Left) Once a bee exits through the escape, she will be unable to get back in. *(Right)* A hive box is provided as near as possible to the blocked entrance to the tree. Finding their entry blocked, the bees will soon take up residence in the hive.

If the opening in the tree is large (say larger than 50 to 100 square inches), you will now have a large surface area of screen over which the bees will be plastered on the inside looking for a way out. One way to speed up their discovery of the bee escape is to cover some or all of the screen with dark cloth except for the area around the bee escape. The bees will quickly move toward the light and once there they will discover the escape. However, having exited the tree, they will find their path to reentry quite effectively blocked.

Next we must provide a home for the bees that have been denied access back into the tree. This is done by placing a standard movable frame commercial hive as close to the blocked opening as possible. For those who are more rustically inclined, a log gum can be used in place of the commercial hive. If the bee tree opening is near the ground, a simple stand of rocks or logs can be improvised for the hive. The stand should be constructed to tilt the hive forward slightly to keep rain water from running into the hive.

If the opening is more than a foot or two off the ground, the hive support stand described in Chapter 3 can be used. Assemble the stand at the desired elevation and be sure to include safety nails through the frame crosspieces for additional insurance against the frame slipping. Next lash the base board in place and adjust the hinged baseboard supports to tilt the baseboard slightly forward, and then place the hive body with frames and cover on to the baseboard. Since the whole assembly must stay in place four to eight weeks, it is important that the hive be securely fastened to withstand buffeting by the wind and swaying of the tree. To insure sturdiness of the assembly, I recommend tack nailing the hive to the base, with two or three nails driven part way in, and then lashing the hive and cover to the baseboard for additional security. The nails can be pulled easily and the lashings can be removed when it later becomes time to bring down the hive.

The frames that are placed in the hive, whether it is on the ground or elevated on the tree, could all contain foundation. However, to get the bees that are locked out of their tree interested in the new hive, it is much better if at least one frame of brood or drawn comb is taken from an established hive. This will attract the bees to the new hive and encourage them to set up housekeeping right away.

Consider now the plight of the bees. They will head out in the morning on their nectar and pollen gathering rounds and upon returning to the tree they will find their reentry blocked. They will buzz around in a confused fashion, cluster around the bee escape in an excited little ball, and form here and there in distracted little knots. Eventually one or two will notice the hive and wander in. Smells nice in there, what with all that foundation and comb. A little more exploring and they'll find the brood comb. Pretty soon a few more will wander in, and after three or four hours there will be some bees collecting nectar and depositing it in the hive box just as though they had lived there all of their lives. At night, most of the bees will retire to the hive box, but during the day many of them will cluster around the bee escape trying to get back into the tree. Why? What's wrong with the hive? What's wrong with the hive is that it doesn't have a queen. So you have to introduce one.

When should the queen be introduced? You should wait until you are sure that the tree is properly sealed and that the bees haven't found a way back into the tree. The first few times you check the tree, you may find that the bees have found some new way into the tree which you will have to seal. However, once the tree is properly sealed, the population in your hive will grow quickly. Some bee hunters like to wait three or four weeks before introducing the queen. I like to introduce her sooner. For one thing, the worker bees only live for six weeks and the bees in that hive are quickly dying off. I like to begin raising new brood as soon as possible. For another thing, a colony of

When locked out of
a tree and thereby
prevented from getting to
their queen, bees will
quickly cluster on a
cage with a queen in it.

queenless bees is a colony of irritable bees and they'll attack more readily. Once a queen is introduced, they will settle down, go inside where they belong, start drawing comb and stop hanging around the bee escape and generally fidgeting about. I find it works well to wait about a week after the tree is sealed before introducing the queen. At that time, if no more than five to ten bees per hour are coming out of the escape, I introduce the queen. If more than five to ten per hour are coming out, I wait a little longer, but in no event more than two weeks.

Queen bees can be ordered by mail or by phone during most of the year from a number of commercial apiaries. Most of these apiaries advertise in bee publications such as *American Bee Journal* and *Gleanings in Bee Culture*, and the bee hunter who needs a queen for his hives will find these apiaries to be quick and convenient sources of supply. When you order a queen to add to your colony, there is no need to try to match the strain of bees that is in the hive. One of the advantages of this method of capturing bees is that it allows you to introduce a queen of the type you want, and then over a period of a few months, as her offspring become the working force of the colony, the colony will gradually be converted to the same strain as the queen that you ordered. So if you want Starline Italians or Midnight caucasians, the time to make up your mind is when you order you queen. When you order a queen, most apiaries will provide two additional services for a slight extra fee. One service is marking of the queen, and the other is clipping one of her wings. When marking the queen the apiarist will put a small dab of bright paint, usually white or yellow, on the thorax of the queen. This makes her much easier to spot when you need to find her, such as during a subsequent requeening. The clipped wing is primarily intended to keep the queen from swarming, but it also helps somewhat in locating her. Both services, clipping and marking, are well worth the small additional price.

There are many subtleties to introducing the queen to the colony. For example, the new queen should be in approximately the same egg laying state as the old queen if she is to be absolutely assured of acceptance. These subtleties are beyond the scope of this book and the bee hunter who is interested in such detail is referred to a standard beekeeping text. Suffice it to say that the colony that has been locked out of its tree, and has taken up queenless housekeeping in a hive box with only one or two frames of brood, is so hungry for a queen that it will accept darn near anything. I am aware of no case of a colony in such a situation rejecting a queen that was offered to it.

The queen will come from the supplier in a small shipping container and the container itself is used to introduce the queen into the colony. The containers typically have two or three compartments, a hole at either end, and one face made of screen. The holes in the ends are plugged with corks, and one of the corks leads into a chamber that is plugged with candy. To introduce the queen to the colony, first pull out the plug that leads to the chamber plugged with candy (the cork at the other end plugs the hole the apiarist used to put the bees in the container and this plug should not be disturbed). Once the cork leading to the candy chamber has been removed, the shipping cage is placed into the hive box. The queen will be shipped along with several worker bees who will tend to her in transit. Some authorities recommend removing the worker bees from the container before placing it in the hive to keep the new bees from fighting with the ones already in the hive. Some authorities say don't bother. Take your pick.

When placing the shipping cage into the colony to introduce the queen, the cage should be placed in the top of the hive between two frames in such a way that the bees in the colony have access to both the screen surface of the case and the opening leading to the chamber plugged with candy. The workers in the colony will, in the course of a day or two, eat their way through the candy, thereby liberating the queen and the workers in the shipping container. By allowing the colony access to the screened surface of the shipping cage, you allow the workers in the colony to acquaint themselves with the queen while the liberation process is going on. Such gradual acquaintance helps insure that the colony will accept their new queen.

Once you have introduced the queen, the first three steps of the capture have been completed, namely: blocking the tree, providing an alternate home, and queening the colony. Over the next few weeks, the colony should be disturbed as little as possible. During this time the bees will be adjusting to their new home and their new queen, drawing comb, raising brood, and doing all those little chores that make a hive a home. If you want to speed the adjustment and settlement process, you can feed your bees. They will greatly appreciate a sugar water solution fed to them in one of the inexpensive bee feeders available from any bee supply house.

The last step, which is to allow the workers back into the tree, can be done as soon as four weeks after the queen is put in the new colony, but it is better to wait six to eight weeks. During this time workers will continue to dribble out of the tree, but there will be fewer and fewer each day as the colony in the tree gets weaker and weaker. For a few weeks, these additional workers will be accepted by the colony outside. But when the outside colony gets strong enough, it will reject them. After three to five weeks, the brood of the new queen will start to emerge, and after six to eight weeks, few if any of the bees in the outside colony will be bees that originally came from the tree. Now you are ready for the last step: allowing your colony access to the tree.

To do this, just remove the screen, dark cloth, bee escape, and any other hole plugging equipment that you may have used to block up the tree. In less time than it takes to tell about it, the bees in your colony will discover the honey in the tree and they will also discover that it is being defended by a very weak colony. They will descend on the colony in the tree and kill any remaining worker bees and the old queen. Then they will start removing the honey, bit by bit and drop by drop. When it comes to cleaning up sweet water or honey, bees are the world's most efficient scavengers. They will not stop until every last scrap of honey is transferred to the new hive. During this phase of the operation, the bee hunter will have to keep a watchful eye on the progress of his bees. Since the bees are working with concentrated honey, the work will go quickly. If there is a lot of honey in the tree, it may be necessary to give the bees additional supers (removable upper story of a hive for storing honey) so they don't run out of

An easy way to introduce the queen to the colony is to staple the queen cage to an elastic, run the elastic around a frame, and put the frame back in the hive. Be sure the workers can get to the screened surface of the cage and be sure the cork is removed from the candy compartment of the cage.

room. Depending on the amount of honey in the tree and the size of the worker force in your colony, it will take anywhere from a day or two to a week or two for your bees to remove all the honey from the tree.

Once your bees are done with the tree, you are done with it also. Without cutting down the tree you have removed all the honey and captured most of the bees with only a few casualties. If you want to insure that the tree is not repopulated by another swarm of bees looking for a home, you will have to seal it up. If that is not a concern, leave the tree as is. You will continue to see occasional bees flying about for a month or so as remaining brood in the tree emerges, but the stragglers in the tree are no longer a viable colony and will soon die out.

Bees that take up residence in rock formations that are not accessible can be captured in exactly the same way as was just described for trees. When plugging up the holes and screening the opening, it may be necessary to do a little stonework and use some mortar. But aside from these mechanical details the overall approach is exactly the same as that just described.

Although the method just described is effective in terms of getting the bees and the honey out of the tree, it has one disadvantage—it's slow. If you have to get the bees out in a hurry, there is

One non-destructive method of capturing bees is to tie a transport box over the opening and block off or plug up all other avenues of escape. The bees can then be driven into the box by banging on the tree or by very heavy smoking. If the opening is too large to be covered by the end of the transport box, cover part of the opening with screen wire. Once the box is in place, it is advisable to cover any screened areas with dark cloth so that the only light the bees see will be coming through the transport box.

another faster way to do it. First seal off all entrances to the tree except for the main entrance. Then place a section of comb in your bee transport box over the entrance being used by the bees and tie up the box. Seal any openings around the box so that the bees have no choice but to go into the box if they come out of the tree. It is best to make the seal around the box light tight so that the only light the bees see will be coming from the screen at the end of the box.

Next, the bees must be driven from the tree. This can be done by heavy smoking, by banging on the tree, or by a combination of the two. Beating on the tree works better on small trees than on large ones since it is difficult to hit on the side of a very big tree hard enough to make it vibrate sufficiently to drive the bees out. On smaller trees, a sledge hammer, the back of an ax, or a stout stick might set up enough commotion to drive the bees out. On larger trees you might have to suspend a short piece of log from a branch with a piece of rope and then swing the log back and forth into the trunk.

If you want to smoke the bees out, it may be necessary to bore a hole for introducing the smoke, or you might be able to use an existing hole. Smoking will also tend to calm the bees down, and it will take a fairly high level of smoking to drive them out.

The smoking or beating on the tree may have to be continued for an hour or more since the bees will leave their home with great reluctance. However, if you can sustain the disturbance long enough to drive out the queen, the others will follow readily. Although I have never done it, I have often wondered how well it would work to tie a queen cage with a queen in it to the screened end of the transport box. This just might make the bees less reluctant to leave and should the queen leave the tree, there could be no immediate fight between the queens since one is protected in a cage.

The bees can be observed through the screened end of the transport box. Once you feel that you have most of them in the box, remove the box, close the lid, and take the bees home to be transferred to a commercial hive or a bee gum. If you want to recover the honey that is in the tree, you can either return to the tree with an established hive and let those bees rob the honey, or you can wait until the bees that you have captured become established in their hive and then return with that colony. In the interim, the hole in the tree can be sealed. This will result in the death of some bees, those you didn't drive out plus those that emerge, but the loss will be minimal if you do an effective job of driving out the bees. By sealing the tree until you bring back another colony to rob it, you can insure that the residual colony in the tree will be as weak as possible before the robbing

The transport box, with a chain or strap handle added, is a convenient container in which to take your bees home.

begins. You will also be insuring that some wild colony doesn't rob the tree before you get back to it.

SEMI-DESTRUCTIVE METHODS

Short of actually cutting the tree down, there are other means of gaining access to the bees and these other means may be more appropriate in certain situations.

For example, in areas where very large trees are common, bees will occasionally be found living in a hollow limb of a large tree. In such a case, first check to make sure that the bees are really living in the limb and that they are not just using the opening in the limb for access into a hollow trunk. If in fact the bees are living in a limb, the limb can be cut off and cut up into gums just as though it were a small tree trunk. In such a case, tie a rope around the limb and lower it gently to the ground to minimize damage to the comb and colony inside. Pruning such a hollow limb off a tree may not be objectionable even in cases where it would be unacceptable to cut down the whole tree, and removing such diseased or rotting wood may actually benefit the tree.

In other cases, it may be possible to use the wedging technique, or a minor modification of it, while the tree is still standing. In large trees (100 inches or more in diameter) it is often possible to split out a section twelve to fifteen inches wide and several feet long without doing any significant damage to the tree. This is particularly true if the area to be split out is already split or rotted, in which case it may be contributing little to the tree structurally or biologically.

Whether you are cutting off a limb or splitting a piece out of the trunk in place, you will have to climb up into the tree to gain access to the area where you plan to work. If the tree is easily climbable, or if the tree is in an area where ladders can easily be brought to it, access is not a problem. But big trees in remote areas can be something of a challenge. Some bee hunters take enough nails and other equipment to the tree that they can construct a ladder up the side of the tree. Others use the spiked attachments that loggers put on their boots to climb trees. With these attachments and a rope wrapped around the tree, it is possible to climb almost any tree. Just one word of caution in this regard. Be sure you know what you are doing. I recently read of an Ohio bee hunter who was scrambling around in a bee tree preparatory to robbin' the bee, lost his footing, and fell some seventy-five feet to his death. When climbing around in tall trees or cutting trees down, keep safety in mind at all times.

BEES IN HOUSES AND OTHER STRUCTURES

When it comes to finding new places to take up residence, honey bees do a pretty thorough job. They check every nook and cranny and every crack and crevice in their search for new quarters. And the cracks and crannies that they check include those in man-made structures. Honey bee colonies are often found in old deserted buildings, usually between outer and inner walls or between floors and ceilings. Occasionally they even make a nuisance of themselves in occupied dwellings.

If you track your bees down and find out that they are living in a building, or if someone asks you to remove a colony of bees from a building and the structure cannot be damaged, the removal can be accomplished in a manner very similar to that described earlier in this chapter for non-destructive removal of bees from a tree. A method is improvised to place a bee escape over the opening being used by the bees. Then an alternate home (hive box) is provided for the bees, later a queen is provided, and then the bees are allowed back into the building to remove the honey. In lieu of a bee escape, it is also possible to use a cone made of common window screen wire. The cone should be

A ladder propped against a house or tree will provide a temporary stand for a hive. Note the wire cone that has been placed over the bees' entrance into the building. The cone will prevent the bees from re-entering the building and they will take up residence in the hive.

about one inch in diameter and open at the small end. The large end should also be open and should be large enough to cover the opening that the bees are using. The large end is then flared and stapled or otherwise fastened over the hole the bees are using. The bees will come out of the hole, walk or fly out the small end of the cone, and upon their return they will be unable to find their way back in. In effect, the cone will serve the same purpose as the bee escape. It is sometimes effective to use a cone in conjunction with a bee escape. In such an application, the bee escape is installed and then the cone is installed over it. Such an installation will keep the bees away from the outside of the bee escape. This is an advantage because the mass of bees that congregates on the outside of the bee escape when the bees are locked out of their home impedes the movement of bees outward through the escape. In a pinch, the large end of a funnel can be fastened over the opening that the bees are using. The funnel will serve much the same purpose as the wire cone since it will allow the bees easy departure from their hole, but will prevent their reentry unless they stumble on the small opening in the end of the funnel.

When bees get into an occupied dwelling, the owner usually reaches for the phone and calls the exterminator. Aside from the distasteful and wasteful aspects of killing all the bees, the idea sometimes backfires. I recently heard of a case where the homeowner called the exterminator and the exterminator promptly came and killed all the bees that had gotten in through a crack in the siding. The bees were living in the space between the ceiling of the first floor and the floor of the second floor. The exterminators killed all the bees all right, but they forgot one thing: the honey. Several days later the homeowner noticed a damp spot in the plaster ceiling of his living room. Every day the spot grew a little bigger. After two weeks the spot was three to four feet in diameter and the plaster was starting to sag. Eventually a plasterer had to be called in, a large section of ceiling was cut out along with a mess of honey and honey comb, and a new ceiling was installed. It was a fairly expensive way to learn that honey bees fan their colonies and bring in water to keep them cool in hot weather. And that fanning and evaporative cooling are what keeps the combs from melting and the honey from running.

SWARMS

Capturing a swarm is not bee hunting in the sense of tracking the bees to their tree. But it's fun. It's a way to get more bees for your apiary, if you want to keep bees. And the presence of swarms can furnish the bee hunter with some useful information for subsequent hunts.

The swarming of bees and the reasons for that swarming are described in Chapter 2. When the bees swarm, they don't go very far from the parent colony before they land and form a ball or knot on a branch, fence, or the side of a house. The swarm usually doesn't travel more than one or two hundred yards before making this first landing, and I have seen cases where the bees went no more than fifty feet. Thus, in addition to providing bees for your apiary, the location of the swarm provides a valuable clue as to where to look for a wild colony, assuming the bees did not issue from someone's apiary.

If you are lucky enough to see a swarm in the air, you will be seeing one of the natural world's most impressive sights. The swirling buzzing black cloud is a sight to see, and it can even be a little unsettling if you are not aware of the fact that swarming bees are extremely gentle. Before leaving their old colony, the bees gorge on honey to provide food and to enable them to make beeswax in their new home. This engorgement on honey makes the bees very docile. As a result, many experienced beekeepers capture swarms using little or no protective equipment. It is probably a good idea for the

Swarms are quite gentle and are easily handled. This interesting old photo shows an enormous swarm that was found in June, 1919, in Indiana. The swarm had issued from one of the hives in the background.

beginner to wear at least a headnet, and if he is really concerned, he should wear a complete complement of protective gear.

How does one capture a swarm? It's fairly easy, but the exact mechanics of the process depend on where the swarm happens to land. If the swarm lands on a branch that is accessible, the branch can be cut off and placed in a transport box or other container and taken home. In one case a neighbor of mine had a swarm in his yard and he asked me to come remove the bees for him. The bees were on a branch in some shrubs, and all I had to do was cut the branch off and carry the branch with the bees on it to my house which was several hundred yards away. Once home, I placed the bees into a commercial hive.

Introducing the bees to the hive is fairly straightforward since the swarm is actively looking for a home. One way to do it is to take the top cover and the inner cover off the hive and then place the swarm on top of the frame. The bees will quickly disperse down between the sheets of foundation. Another way to do it is to rest the swarm at the entrance to the hive. They will soon discover the nice safe home nearby and run inside. If you place the swarm at the entrance to the hive, place a tarpaulin or a piece of plywood down in front of the hive to keep the bees from getting tangled up in the grass.

You may wish to place a frame of drawn comb, honey, or brood in the hive before introducing the swarm, but this is not absolutely necessary. If the bees are to be placed in a bee gum, remove the cover from the gum and shake the bees off the branch, and into the gum. Once the bees are inside, replace the cover.

Often swarms will land on a branch which can be cut off and easily transported. However, swarms are not always that cooperative. Sometimes one will land on a solid object, such as this gravestone, in which case it will have to be scraped off into a transport box or a hive if it is to be captured.

Sometimes the swarm won't cooperate by landing on a branch that can easily be cut off. They may land on the side of a house, on a fence, or on some other object. In such cases the bees must be shaken or scraped into a box, bag, or other container. The swarm will tolerate quite a bit of handling, and some beekeepers perform this operation with their bare hands; but I recommend that you use a brush, wear gloves, or both. If the bees are high in a tree on an inaccessible branch, some beekeepers will throw a rope over the branch by means of a weight tied to the end of the rope. A large burlap or cheesecloth sack is then propped open, secured to the end of a pole, and held under the swarm. A good hard shake will usually suffice to dislodge the swarm and cause it to fall into the sack.

Some people contend that if you came across a swarm that is in the air, or the swarm takes off before you get positioned to capture it, you can get the swarm to land by banging on a pan, ringing a bell, or blowing an automobile horn. Supposedly these loud noises interfere with the ability of the swarm to hear the piping of the queen, and thereby confuse and disorient the swarm causing it to land. There is some controversy as to the effectiveness of this technique, but if the swarm is in the air it sure can't hurt to try.

One last note with regard to swarms. You may wonder how you will ever be lucky enough to just happen upon a swarm. The answer is that unless you have an apiary or a number of bee trees right near you, you probably won't just happen on one. The trick is to have people notify you of swarms around their homes and farms. There are two ways to do this. First, tell your friends and acquaintances that you are interested in bees and would like to be notified of any swarms. Second, give your local police and fire departments the same information. Police and fire departments are often called upon by individuals who want assistance removing swarms from their property and these agencies are usually quite happy to turn the problem over to a local beekeeper who will handle it for them.

9. Transporting and Transferring Bees

If the Lord delight in us, then he will bring us into this land and give it to us, a land which flowereth with milk and honey.

NUMBERS 14:8

The methods described in the previous chapters left you with bees in one of three containers. If you cut the tree into gums, the bees are in short sections of hollow tree; if you wedged the tree or drove the bees into a transport box, they are in a transport box; and if you trapped them out of the tree and provided a hive for them, they are now in a hive box. And now they must be moved to the place where you want to keep them permanently. If they are not already in their permanent home, they must be transferred to the hive or bee gum in which you want to keep them.

BEE GUMS

The precautions to be observed when transporting bee gums were described in Chapter 7. Once you get the bees home, you will have to decide whether you want to keep them in the gum or in a standard commercial hive. The standard hive is much easier to manage and you will get bigger, healthier colonies and much better honey production if the bees are placed in a commercial hive than you will if they are kept in a gum. The gum, on the other hand, is a nostalgic piece of

When moving sections of bee gum, avoid rough treatment in order to minimize damage to the comb inside.

Americana and, if it is a large one with few improvements, it will provide your backyard or apiary with a genuine element of the natural. The bees in that gum will live, behave, and look just as they would have in the wild.

Set your bee gum up on a board that is elevated off the ground on some bricks, logs, or cinder blocks. Other improvements that can be made to the gum are described in Chapter 3.

If the hollow area in the gum is so small that it crowds the bees, two things can be done. One is to add another section of gum to the top or bottom of the gum with the bees, thereby giving them more space. The other thing that can be done is to add a standard super to the top of the gum. This will give the bees the additional space in the super to store their honey and, since the super will have moveable frames, the honey will be much easier to extract than if the bees were storing it in the gum. To add a super to the top of a gum, first cut the top of the gum off square if it is not already square. Then cut a piece of exterior plywood or fasten together some pieces of board so that you have a platform the size of the bottom of the super that is to be added to the gum (approximately seventeen inches by twenty-one inches for a standard super). Next cut a hole in the center of the wooden platform and make the hole approximately the same size as the hole in the center of the gum. The platform is then nailed to the top of the gum. Any supers that are to be added can then be stacked on top of the platform. The bees will tend to use the gum as a brood chamber and will store honey in the super, which is just what you want.

If you want to get the bees out of a gum altogether and into a standard hive, you can either split the gum open and physically remove them, or you can blow the bees out of the gum using a bee blower or a shop vacuum hooked up as a blower. In either case, smoke the bees beforehand and wait three to five minutes after the smoking to insure that they have calmed down.

When splitting the gum, proceed carefully so that as little damage as possible is done to the comb inside. The pieces of comb can then be removed from the gum (much to the bees' displeasure) and the bees can be brushed directly into the hive if the cover and inner cover are removed. If you have just brought the gum home and you are not sure whether or not the queen is in the gum, place a queen excluder on top of the hive, and then place an empty hive body on top of the excluder and brush the bees onto the queen excluder. Most of the bees will go past the queen excluder and down into the lower hive body, but the queen will be unable to do so. She will be trapped above the excluder where a small knot of bees will begin to congregate around her. As soon as you see this cluster forming, ascertain that you do have the queen. Then remove the upper hive body and gently turn the queen excluder upside down and allow the queen and her attendants to run into the hive.

Any brood comb that is found in the gums should be returned to the bees. This is done by placing the sections of brood comb in empty frames (no foundation) and holding the pieces of comb in place with elastic bands. These frames of brood comb are then placed in the hive into which you are placing your bees.

Before returning the brood comb to the bees, examine it carefully and you will be privileged to observe what, for any beekeeper, is a very satisfying sight—the birth of a bee. Here and there around the brood comb you will see worker cells that are just starting to open. In some cases slight movement will be visible inside. In other cases the bee's feelers will be protruding out of the cell. In still other cases a head or shoulders will be protruding. Watch one of these cells for a few minutes and you will see the bee struggle. And rest. And struggle some more. And eventually, out she'll pop. A new worker has just joined the work force where she will help maintain the viability of the colony.

If the gum from which you are removing the bees is short enough, the bees can be blown out of the gum and into the hive. To do so, place a board with a hole in it over the top of the hive. The hole should be slightly larger than the inside diameter of the gum. Place

When transferring bees from a gum into a commercial hive, place their brood comb in empty frames in the hive. The comb can be held in the frames with elastic bands.

the gum on top of the hive and centered over the hole in the board. Using a bee blower or a shop vacuum, blow the bees out of the gum and into the hive. Place a piece of screen over the hive entrance so the bees don't get blown out of the gum, through the hive, and out onto the grass. The bees will resist being blown out of the gum and will cling to the sides of the gum and to the comb. As the bees at the upper end of the gum are blown down, tear or cut the upper piece of comb out of the gum and blow off the bees into the gum. Continue to work down through the gum in this manner, and soon you will have all the bees in the hive (except for those that are flying around). If you want to check for the presence of a queen, place a queen excluder over the hive before putting the board with the hole in it on top of the hive. Check frequently for the presence of the queen on the excluder. Once she is found, release her into the hive and remove the queen excluder, and the rest of the blowing operation will go much easier.

TRANSPORT BOXES

If you wedged the tree, or if you drove the bees out into a transport box, you are now confronted with the problem of transferring the bees into the hive. The bees should be removed from the transport box fairly quickly, since unlike the bee gum, the box does not offer suitable living quarters for your bees. Quick removal is particularly important if the bees in the box are a captured swarm. Swarming bees load up on honey before they swarm and they are ready to start making comb at the slightest excuse. If left in the box, even just overnight, there is a good chance the bees will start making comb.

The bee hunter wants to have this comb drawn in the bee's new home and not wasted in the transport box.

To transfer the bees, prepare a board similar to that used when blowing bees out of a gum, except that the hole in the center should be square rather than round to accommodate the square opening of the bee box. Open the lid of the bee box slightly, slide a thin piece of cardboard under the lid to keep the bees from flying out, and then open the lid all the way. Next turn the box upside down over the opening in the board on top of the hive and slide out the piece of cardboard. At this point the bees will have access to the hive and some will move down voluntarily. The majority, however, will have to be blown out. The end of the transport box that is facing up at this point is the screened end and the bees can be blown through the screen out of the box and down into the hive. As was the case when the bees were being blown out of the gum, place a piece of screen over the hive entrance to keep the bees from being blown right out of the hive. Also, a few frames of drawn comb or foundation will help insure your bees' acceptance of their new home, and a queen excluder can be used to check for the presence of a queen.

If there are no pieces of comb or foundation in the transport box, and if the bees are fairly calm, it may be possible to take the cover and the inner cover off your hive and just shake the bees out to the top of the frames. They will quickly run down between the pieces of foundation.

STANDARD HIVES

If you used the non-destructive methods described in Chapter 8, you may already have your bees in a standard hive depending on which method you used. However, when we left the effort in Chapter 8, the hive was still beside the house or the tree where the bees were captured. The problem now is to get the hive home.

How the hive relocation effort should proceed depends on how far the hive is to be moved, and movements can be classified as short (up to a few hundred feet), intermediate (a few hundred feet to three or four miles), and long (over four miles).

If a hive is picked up and relocated a few hundred feet, many of the bees will fly out of the hive, make their rounds, and then return to the former location of the hive. There they will mill about, and many will never find their way to the new hive location. In all probability, they will either join another colony or die. The bee hunter who is moving his colony cannot tolerate this sad state of affairs since the working force of the colony represents a large portion

Bees can be blown from
a transport box into a hive.
Over the hive place a
wooden cover with a square
hole in it. Then place
the transport box upside
down over the hole and
blow the bees out,
using a bee blower or a
shop vacuum hooked
up as a blower.

Bees can be blown from a bee gum into a hive box in much the same manner that they can be blown from the transport box into the box.

of the total population, and loss of the working force would be a major setback to the colony. One way to prevent this loss of the work force is to relocate the hive gradually. If the moves are no more than three to five feet at a time, the bees will adjust. Another useful device is to lean a board up against the front of the hive once it has been moved. The bees will then have to fly around the board on their way out of the hive. This will confuse them, so before departing, they will fly in circles around the hive to get their bearings. In so doing they will get a fix on the new location of the hive, thus making their return to the proper spot more certain.

Another way to prevent loss upon relocation of the hive is to place an empty hive body at the former location of the colony once the colony is moved. Those bees that return to the former location will gather in the empty hive. The empty hive must periodically (at least once a day) be picked up and taken to the new location where the bees in it are reunited with the main colony. This can be done by shaking the bees onto a piece of tarpaulin in front of the colony, or by lifting the covers off the main colony and shaking or brushing the stragglers onto the tops of the frames.

If the bees are to be moved a long distance (over four miles), there is no danger of their returning to their former homesite. The real problem in this case is care for the bees during the movement operation itself. Unlike the professional beekeeper, the bee hunter will rarely find himself in a position where he has to move his bees so far that it involves overnight travel. This simplies the problem.

To prepare the colony for a long move, place a piece of screen over the entrance to seal the bees into the hive. This should be done early in the morning or late in the evening when the field force is back in the hive. Do not entirely block the entrance off, as with a piece of wood, since the bees will need air circulation during the trip. Fasten the hive bodies together and fasten the bottom hive to the base board to insure that the elements of the hive assembly don't shift relative to one another, since such shifting might allow the bees to escape. Bee supply houses sell special staples that are intended for use in stapling hive assembles together for movement. If these are not available, boards can be nailed to the sides and back of the hives, thereby fastening all the parts together.

During movement of the hives, try to avoid prolonged exposure to direct sunlight and allow air to circulate freely over the hives. Do not enclose them in an area such as a closed trunk where the air will be close and hot and may even contain exhaust fumes. Avoid unnecessary jarring or shaking of the hives since this could cause damage to the combs inside.

Once the bees are in their new location, they can be released with little fear of their return to the former location of the hive. It is, however, still a good idea to lean a board against the front of the hive to cause the bees to circle when they leave, thereby getting a fix on the new location of their home.

Moves in the intermediate range (a few hundred feet to three or four miles) are the trickiest. There is a distinct danger that the bees will return to their old home. Yet moving the hive a mile or two at the rate of three or four feet a day is somewhat impractical, and placing an empty hiving body at the old location and emptying it one or two times a day is only slightly less inconvenient. I have found the best way to move such hives is to just wait for the cold weather of late fall or winter when no bees are flying, put a piece of screen over the entrance, and move the bees. Once they are in their new location and have been there for a few days the piece of screen can be removed and there need be little fear of loss of bees.

Another way to make such a move is to move the bees from their original location to a temporary location that is at least three to four miles from both the original location and the proposed final location. Once the bees have been in the temporary location for three or four weeks, they can be moved to their final location and there will be no need to worry about them returning to either of the former locations.

10. Processing Honey and Beeswax

And still more, later flowers to the bees,
Until they think summer will never cease,
For summer has o'er-brimmed their clammy cells.

JOHN KEATS c. 1819
To Autumn

Some bee hunters will stop their hunting activities at the point of locating and marking the tree. Most, however, will use one of the methods described in Chapter 7 or Chapter 8 to actually remove the honey from the tree. If the tree was split, the bee hunter now has one or more buckets of honey and comb that need to be processed. If the tree was cut into gums, the comb must be removed from the gums and processed. And if one of the non-destructive methods of Chapter 8 was used, the honey and bees will now be in a commercial hive. If the honey is in a commercial hive, conventional honey extraction techniques can be used and these methods are described in any standard beekeeping text. This chapter will concentrate on the problems of the bee hunter. And we will concentrate on saving both the honey and the beeswax.

BEE GUMS

If the bee tree was cut up into gums, the bee hunter must first remove the honey comb from the gums and place it in buckets or pots for subsequent processing.

If the gums are not to be saved to keep bees in, the easiest way

To split a section of bee gum, stand the gum on end and drive two wedges into opposite sides.

A gum that is split open reveals the flat layers of comb the way the bees made them in their natural state.

to get the comb out is to stand the gum on end and split it with an ax or a pair of log spitting wedges. Once the gum is split, lay the two halves flat on the ground, tear out the pieces of comb and place them in a clean bucket. The splitting operation, or the original cutting operation in the woods, may have resulted in a lot of spilled honey in the pieces of the gum. This honey should be spooned out and placed in the bucket also. Try to avoid getting any more sawdust, wood chips, and other contaminants into the honey than is absolutely necessary. But don't worry about it if you get some in; it's inevitable. The honey will have to be strained later anyway.

If you have been keeping your bees in a bee gum and want to remove the honey without destroying the gum, a slightly different procedure must be followed. The bee gum is left upright on its stand and the comb is removed in place. Once the outer cover is removed, the next step is to detach the comb from the inner cover. (See Chapter 3 for a description and photos of a bee gum that has been improved for permanently keeping bees.) This is done by slipping a long bladed knife under the inner cover and working around the gum until all of the comb has been cut loose. Then lift off the inner cover.

Recall that there are two crossed sticks about halfway down the gum. The comb below these sticks will contain brood and should be left in place. The comb above the sticks will contain mostly honey, and it is this comb that the bee hunter wants to remove with minimum damage. The comb in the upper chamber is best removed by reaching down between the pieces of comb with a long tool or knife and cutting or tearing the bottom of the comb loose from the crossed sticks. The tool or knife that is used for this purpose should have a 90° bend at the end to enable you to cut across the bottom of the comb just above the crossed sticks. Once this is done, the slab of comb can be pulled out with a little wiggling and twisting.

When removing comb from bee gums, keep the following points in mind:

- If the bees are smoked a few minutes before the removal begins, it makes the job much easier.
- If the weather is warm and bees are flying, keep the honey pot covered or it will soon be filled with bees trying to recover their honey.
- If you pull out any comb that has brood in it rather than honey, return it to the bees. If it's part brood and part honey, the comb can be cut and just the brood returned.
- Whether you smoke the bees or not, suit up with protective clothing. Don't expect the bees to be wildly enthusiastic about the honey removal operation. If the truth must be told, it tends to displease them.

PROCESSING HONEY

The beekeeper who keeps his bees in standard moveable frame hives can use certain mechanized extraction techniques that are not suitable to the bee hunter. This is so because the mechanized extraction

To remove the inner
cover from a bee gum,
slip the blade of a
long knife under the
cover to cut loose
the comb.

When removing comb
from a bee gum, a tool
such as this is very
handy. It can be
inserted from above,
between the sheets of
comb, and then
turned sideways to
cut off the sheets so
that they can be removed.

Use a sharp knife to
cut the comb loose
from the split section
of gum. Once the comb
is cut free, it will lift
out in large, flat slabs.

This tray of comb has
been cut out of a
gum and is ready for
processing. It should
not be left uncovered for
very long, or the bees
will steal all the
honey out of it.

A long tool or knife must be slipped between the sheets of comb in the gum to cut the comb loose from its attachment points. Once the comb is cut loose, it will lift out of the gum in flat sheets.

The honey comb that is recovered from a bee tree is often irregular in shape and damaged. The easiest way to process such comb is to crush it by hand and let it drain through a strainer.

techniques depend on the fact that the honey comb from commercial hives is in flat slabs in frames of uniform geometry. In addition to insuring uniform geometry, the frames provide support during the extraction process. The bee hunter, on the other hand, has irregular pieces of broken comb, some of which is in nice flat pieces and some of which isn't, to say nothing of the loose honey containing bits of beeswax and wood in the bottom of his pail.

To process his honeycomb, the bee hunter must actually break up the comb and crush it in such a way that all of the cells are broken open thereby releasing the honey. Some people place the honeycomb in a large colander or strainer, crush it with some implement such as a potato masher, and allow the honey to run into a pot or crock below the strainer. I find it more effective to crush the comb in my hands while holding it over the strainer. Once the comb is crushed, leave the pieces of beeswax in the strainer to drain for several hours. This operation should be done in a warm place, 70°F or higher, since the viscosity of honey increases quickly as the temperature drops. The warmer it is, the more readily the honey will flow from the crushed wax.

Once the wax is drained, lay it aside for further processing. Take any pails or buckets that have loose honey in them and allow them to drain through the strainer. Once this is done, step one of the straining process is done.

Step two consists of running the honey through a finer mesh filter to get out any remaining pieces of beeswax or other contaminants. Filter material is available from commercial bee supply houses, but the bee hunter who is processing relatively small quantities of honey will find that ordinary cheesecloth works quite satisfactorily. An easy way to do this filtering is to get an oversized funnel and line it with at least four layers of cheesecloth. Pour the honey into the funnel and let it drain directly into sterilized Mason jars or other containers in which you plan to store it.

A word is in order at this point about pollen and beeswax in the honey. Both pollen and beeswax are edible high-protein foods. Small amounts of either left in the honey will not impair its healthfulness nor its flavor. Pollen is sold in some health food stores, and it is not uncommon to find small amounts of pollen floating in a thin layer on the top of the jars of honey sold in supermarkets. The pollen is so fine that it is virtually impossible to filter it all out. If you find it objectionable, there are two things you can do to minimize the amount of pollen in your honey. First, be selective about which comb you crush into the strainer. Reject any pieces that have a lot of pollen stored in them, and carefully trim away the pollen laden portions of any comb that you do crush. Secondly, if the honey is allowed to stand at room temperature for several days, most of the pollen will rise to the surface where it can be spooned out.

The healthfulness of beeswax as a food is attested to by the fact that some honey is marketed while it's still in the beeswax comb. This honey, known as bulk, chunk, or cut comb honey, is intended to be eaten beeswax and all. These forms of honey are not as available on the commercial market as they once were because of the difficulty of producing and handling these forms of honey. When eaten, the honeycomb can either be broken up in bite-sized chunks, or it can be spread on hot breads and other hot foods, in which case the beeswax turns to liquid. With the resurgence of popularity of organic and natural foods, we may see increased interest in beeswax as a high-protein health food.

Some bee hunters process their honey by heating the combs in an oven. If the temperature is carefully regulated to about 160°F, the beeswax will melt and rise to the top, and the honey will remain below. I strongly recommend against this practice. The ingredients in honey that give it much of its flavor and aroma are very volatile and are easily driven off when the honey is heated. Most commercial beekeepers do heat the honey somewhat in processing it, but they do it under carefully controlled conditions. Even so, enough people feel that this heating adversely affects the honey's taste and aroma that there is a substantial market for raw or unheated honey. Note that the above squeezing method does not require heating the honey at any time during the process.

RENDERING THE BEESWAX

The bee hunter will want to recover as much beeswax as possible from the comb that he collects. Beeswax has a commercial value and currently sells for between $1.50 and $2.50 per pound. The bee hunter can also use the beeswax to make candles for attracting bees (see Chapter 3). Finally, beeswax is useful to the outdoorsman for other purposes, such as dressing bowstrings.

Rendering is the process whereby the beeswax is separated from the undesirable portion of the comb. The undesirable residue consists of pollen, cocoons, brood, and other contaminants. This residue is referred to by beekeepers as slumgum. All methods of rendering the beeswax involve heating it in some way. One method consists of taking the squeezed-out comb and other miscellaneous pieces of comb in a covered container and placing it in an oven to heat at 160-170°F. One disadvantage of this method is that if the wax is

Crushed honey comb can be effectively filtered by straining
it through four layers of cheesecloth.

Home-processed tulip-poplar honey; sweet, robust, and dark.

Honey that has been packed with pieces of comb in the package
or jar is sold as comb, cut comb, or chunk honey, and is available
in some supermarkets and health-food stores.

When beeswax is processed by the submerged sack method, a
layer of wax will form on top of the water as it cools. Note the
difference in color of the wax. Lighter wax sells for a higher price.

over-heated (about 185°F or more) it tends to darken. Another disadvantage is that if the pot is taken out of the oven and allowed to cool,
the bottom layer of the beeswax will entrap a lot of slumgum as it
solidifies. The mess can be poured through a heated strainer while it
is still hot, but this is awkward and messy. A final disadvantage of
this method is that the heated slumgums give off an unpleasant
odor, and if the oven you are using is in your kitchen, you stand a
good chance of stinking up the whole house.

People who keep bees as a hobby often use a solar extractor to render their beeswax. The solar extractor is a box-like device with a glass top that is set out in the sun for heating purposes. The pieces of wax that are to be rendered are placed in the extractor where they are melted. As it melts and runs off, the wax is separated from the residue.

This method of extraction works well for the beekeeper because he is generally working with fairly pure wax, referred to as cappings. The bee hunter, on the other hand, is confronted with a mixture of old comb and new comb with a variety of contaminants in it. The best way to render this beeswax is the submerged sack method. The comb is placed in a bag of double thickness cheesecloth, along with a rock or two for weight. The sack is then placed in a pot of boiling water. The boiling water is hot enough to melt the beeswax which flows out thorugh the pores in the sack and floats to the surface. The sack should be agitated with a stick while it is being boiled to help release the wax. After the sack has boiled for fifteen or twenty minutes, the pot should be removed from the fire and allowed to cool. The wax will form a hardened disc on top of the water as it cools, after which it is easily removed since beeswax shrinks slightly as it cools.

When rendering beeswax, keep the following in mind:

- Don't heat beeswax over an open flame (except by the submerged sack method) because of the fire hazard.
- Sometimes overheated honey is produced as a byproduct of wax rendering. Feed it to the bees.
- Don't boil the beeswax for more than fifteen or twenty minutes, and don't let it boil violently.
- Do not heat beeswax in containers of iron, brass, copper, or zinc as discoloration of the wax might result.
- Don't do the rendering around bee colonies unless you want a lot of company.
- If you have a lot of comb to render, separate the light-colored comb from the dark, since light beeswax is more valuable.

Candlemaking is an art unto itself, and a detailed discussion of the ins and outs of making molded and dipped candles is well beyond the scope of this book. However, the following procedure should serve the purposes of the bee hunter who needs a pure beeswax candle to attract bees.

First, a mold of some type is needed. A great variety of cans, jars, and cartons will suffice, but I find empty pint and quart milk cartons to be especially useful. Cut the top off the carton so it is square and punch a small hole in the bottom center of the carton. Push a piece of candle wick through the hole, tie a knot in the bottom, and pull it up through the carton. Lay a pencil or twig across the top of the cartoon and tie the wick to it.

Heat the beeswax by placing it inside the container and into a pot of boiling water. This jerry-rigged double boiler will keep the wax from burning. Once the wax has melted, pour it into the carton and then set the carton aside to cool. After the wax has cooled thoroughly, peel away the carton and you will find inside a beeswax candle quite adequate for bee hunting.

The wick that is needed can be bought in many hobby stores. For candles under two inches in diameter use a number 3 or 4 wick; over two inches in diameter use number 5 or 6.

STORING HONEY AND BEESWAX

Beeswax is easy to store. Just keep it below its 149°F melting point and don't let the wax moths get into it. The wax moth problem can be eliminated by storing the wax in a sealed jar or box. If further protection is desired, a few drops of ethylene dibromide can be added to the jar or box, or the wax can be frozen. Wax moths and their larvae cannot withstand freezing temperatures.

As foods go, honey is quite easy to store. Because of the high acidity of honey, most bacteria cannot live in it. As a result, there are only two real storage problems: fermentation and granulation.

The fermentation problem can be licked by storing the honey at temperatures below 60°F, or below 50°F if absolute insurance is desired. Fermentation can also be precluded by heating the honey to 145°F for thirty minutes since this kills the yeasts that cause fermentation. Provided the honey is not recontaminated with yeasts after it is heated, it will not ferment no matter how long it is stored. However, the dangers of heating honey were described earlier, so unless you have large quantities to store, it is better to simply store it below 50°F.

Granulation of honey is caused by precipitation of the dextrose out of the honey solution. Granulated honey is still good to eat, and in fact some honey is marketed that way. Should your honey granulate and should you want to reliquefy it, heat it at 145-150°F for as long as it is necessary to dissolve the crystals. The temperature range of 50-60°F is particularly favorable to the granulation of honey; lower temperatures tend to retard granulation.

Honey can be frozen solid indefinitely with no deterioration in quality, and will neither ferment nor granulate when so frozen.

11. Honey Cookery

My son, eat thou honey, because it is good; and the honey-comb, which is sweet to thy taste.

PROVERBS 24:13

Thou didst eat fine flour, and honey, and oil: and thou wast exeeding beautiful . . .

EZEKIEL 16:13

During the decade of the 1970s, man became increasingly aware of and sensitive to the volume of chemicals that he was dumping into the environment. It turned out that his newly awakened concern was well-founded since in many cases he wound up eating, drinking, or breathing those very chemicals. One offshoot of this sense of concern has been the great increase in popularity in recent years of organic and natural foods. And since there is no food more natural than honey, the popularity of honey has also surged during this same period.

There are several reasons why honey is widely acclaimed by diet-conscious people and natural food advocates. For one thing, honey is in every sense a "natural" sweetener. It requires an absolute minimum of processing. If you buy a jar of honey in the supermarket, there has probably been nothing more done to it than filtering it to get out wax particles, and heating it to kill the yeast spores that might otherwise cause fermentation. There have been no coloring agents added, no preservatives, and no other chemicals of any type other than what the flower and the bee put there to begin with. Since even carefully controlled heating has some effect on the flavor and

169

aroma of honey, some people prefer unheated (and in some cases unfiltered) honey, which is available in many supermarkets as "raw" honey. Honey is such a natural food that it really requires no processing at all. One can break off chunks of filled honeycomb just as the bee produced it and eat those chunks, wax, honey, and all. Honey with the comb included is available in some supermarkets and health food stores as comb, cut comb, or chunk honey. It is not found in these forms as frequently as it is in the form of liquid (extracted) honey because of the greater effort and expense involved in producing and packaging the comb forms of honey.

Another reason for the popularity of honey with diet-conscious persons is that the sugars in honey are in a simple chemical form that is easily used by the body. The sugar in a bag of common white cane sugar is mostly in the form of sucrose. Sucrose is a fairly complicated molecule that must be broken down by the body's digestive system before it can absorbed by the blood. In recent years, there has been some concern expressed that sucrose is in whole, or in part, responsible for a number of ailments. The degree of responsibility that sucrose has for these various ailments remains to be proven conclusively, but the mere suspicion of sugar's guilt has led many people to look for alternate sweeteners.

The sugars in honey, on the other hand, are primarily simple sugars or monosaccharides. Levulose (fruit sugar) and destrose (grape sugar) account for approximately 75 percent of honey by weight. Sucrose makes up less than two percent. Most of the balance is water. The simple sugars in honey are readily absorbed into the blood. Athletes have long made use of this fact by taking honey during competition as a source of quick energy.

Many people think of honey as nothing more than a spread or syrup that can be used on pancakes, toast, muffins, and the like. Nothing could be further from the truth. In the hands of a skillful chef, honey becomes a general purpose sweetener that can be used in place of sugar in many recipes. Through proper utilization, honey can be made to add its own distinctive flavor to the recipe, or it can be used simply as a sweetening agent.

This is not to say that honey can be mindlessly employed in place of sugar in every recipe. Honey works best in such applications as breads, pastries, glazes, pie fillings, custards, pound cakes, ice cream, and in syrups for canning fruit. It does not do as well in light fluffy cakes that have to rise a lot. And the cook must keep in mind that different honeys have distinctly different flavors. In a recipe where the cook wants to use the honey as a sweetening agent only, or where the honey flavor is to be very subtle, it would be inappropriate to use a strong flavored honey such as buckwheat or eucalyptus.

There are certain general rules that the cook should keep in mind when using honey as a sweetener. Whenever honey is being substituted for sugar in a recipe, two-thirds of a cup of honey should be used to replace one cup of sugar. Furthermore, since honey contains some water, whereas normal granulated sugar does not, the cook should reduce the amount of other liquids used in the recipe by one-quarter of a cup for each cup of honey used. To get the honey to run freely out of the measuring cup, use the same cup that was used to measure the shortening, or else put a light coat of vegetable oil in the cup. A rubber spatula will be helpful in getting the last reluctant drops of honey from the measuring cup. When baking, limit temperatures to 350°F to avoid scorching the honey. Such scorching may make the final product too brown.

One final precaution about cooking with honey. No one, even a confirmed honey eater, wants every dish to taste like honey! It is possible to cook an entire meal from appetizer to dessert using honey in every dish and in every dressing without the diner being consciously aware of the taste of honey, except in those cases where the chef wants him to be aware. But it takes a little skill and practice, and in the early stages of experimentation, it is best to err on the side of too little rather than too much honey. With that final precaution, here are the recipes. These recipes were deliberately chosen to show the great versatility of honey as an ingredient in everything from the main course and the dessert to the wine and the salad dressing. The sampling of recipes given here is by no means complete, and the reader who is interested in more recipes and greater detail is referred to the list of honey cookbooks and pamphlets at the end of this chapter.

PEGGY ANN'S GRANOLA

We'll start off our recipes with the run-away favorite health food of the last ten years—granola. Eat it as a breakfast cereal or eat it dry as a snack. Either way it's healthful and delicious.

4	cups Quick Quaker oats
½	cup coarsely chopped unsalted cashew nuts
½	cup coarsely chopped unsalted almonds
½	cup coarsely chopped unsalted hazel nuts
½	cup hulled unsalted sunflower seeds
½	cup sesame seeds
1	cup raw wheat germ

¾	cup soy oil
¾	cup raw honey
1	teaspoon vanilla
½	cup raisins
½	cup chopped dates

Preheat oven to 325°F. Combine oats, nuts, sunflower seeds, sesame seeds and wheat germ in a large bowl. Heat and stir oil, honey, and vanilla until well blended. Pour this mixture over the dry ingredients and mix thoroughly. Spread evenly on a large cookie sheet. Toast 20-25 minutes. Stir frequently. Remove from oven, cool and add raisins and dates. Can be used as a cereal or snack. To store, keep in tightly covered container. Can be stored in refrigerator.

HONEY BUTTER

This stuff is so good it's sinful, and it's so easy to make that even I can do it. Around our house, we use margarine in place of butter in most recipes to hold down on the cholesterol. But this recipe is one place where we indulge. There is something about the subtle mixing of the honey and butter flavors that is just out of this world. You can, however, use an equal amount of margarine in place of the butter listed below.

½	cup butter
½	cup wild honey (or ⅓ cup robust honey)

Allow the honey and butter to come to room temperature and then mix thoroughly. Keep refrigerated until used. When used, it tastes and spreads better if it's again allowed to warm up. If subsequently allowed to warm, it may need occasional remixing. Variations can be made by adding lemon juice, orange juice, or cinnamon to taste.

GLAZED PORK LOIN ROAST

Now we'll try some main courses.

1	(6-pound) pork loin roast	½	cup wine vinegar
1	can (19 ounce) cling peach halves	1	stick (3 inch)
	Peach syrup, drained from halves		cinnamon
¼	cup fresh orange juice	½	teaspoon dry mustard

Drain peaches, reserving syrup. In saucepan, stir together peach syrup, orange juice, wine vinegar and honey. Add cinnamon stick. Bring to boil, lower heat and simmer about 10 minutes, or until clear and thick, stirring. Remove cinnamon stick. Mix a little of the syrup with mustard for a smooth paste. Blend into remaining syrup. Add peaches and let stand until ready to use. Remove ½ cup of syrup to glaze pork loin during the last 30 minutes of roasting. Serve roast with peach halves.

Have meat cut almost free from backbones. Place roast, fat side up, in roasting pan. Heat oven to 325° (moderate). Roast covered, allowing 35 minutes per pound or until meat thermometer registers from 170-180°. About 30 minutes before end of roasting time, spoon glaze from peaches. (Courtesy of California Honey Advisory Board)

GLAZED SKILLET CHICKEN

Here's one for those of you with a few extra chickens running around in the yard.

1	frying chicken (about 3 pounds), cut in serving pieces
	Salt and pepper
¼	cup salad oil
¼	cup mild-flavored honey
¼	cup fresh lemon juice
¼	teaspoon paprika
½	teaspoon dry mustard

Wipe chicken pieces well with damp paper towels. Season with salt and pepper. Heat salad oil in 10-inch skillet. Place chicken, skin side down, in skillet. Brown on one side, turn and brown on other side. Cover and cook over medium heat 15 minutes. Mix together balance of ingredients. Pour over chicken, turning to coat. Continue cooking, uncovered, about 20 minutes. Baste frequently to glaze. Chicken is done when it is fork tender. Makes 4 servings.

TO BAKE IN OVEN: Heat oven to 375° (moderate). Arrange chicken pieces, skin side down in shallow greased baking pan. Brush with marinade. Cover pan with foil. Bake 30 minutes. Remove foil. Turn chicken and brush with marinade. Increase heat to 400°. Bake 15 to 20 minutes until golden brown and tender. (Courtesy of California Honey Advisory Board)

BEEF LOAF IN THE ROUND

This one is guaranteed to stick to your ribs (as if most of us don't have more than enough stuck to our ribs already).

¾	cup milk
1	envelope (1⅜ ounce) onion soup mix
1	egg
1½	cups soft bread crumbs
1½	pound lean ground beef
¼	cup hot catsup
1	tablespoon prepared mustard
2	tablespoons honey
4	slices Monterey Jack cheese
	Noodles or rice

In mixing bowl, combine milk, onion soup mix, lightly beaten egg and bread crumbs. Let stand 5 minutes. Add beef and mix well. Shape mixture in oiled 9-inch ring mold. Turn out onto shallow baking pan. Brush on catsup mixed with mustard and honey. Bake 40 minutes in 400° oven (hot). Brush occasionally with catsup mixture. Remove from oven. Arrange cheese over loaf. Return to oven. Bake about 5 minutes or until cheese melts. Serve with cooked noodles or rice. Makes about 6 servings. (Courtesy of California Honey Advisory Board)

SPINACH SALAD ALÁ MARGARET

This one has about six thousand variations. Here's one variation as a point of departure. If you're on a diet, it's a main course. Otherwise, it can be an appetizer.

½	cup apple cider vinegar
½	cup honey
3	tablespoons catsup
1	tablespoon lemon juice

(combine and shake well)

Arrange a bed of fresh spinach (bite size pieces) on a salad plate. Garnish with quartered hard boiled egg, julienne slices of cheddar cheese and swiss cheese, and crumbled bacon. Serve with the dressing.

DRESSING FOR FRUIT SALAD

Here's a great dressing for a light noontime meal of fresh fruit.

Mix equal parts of salad oil, lemon juice and clover honey. Shake well before using and store in refrigerator. Serve on any fresh fruits such as apples, pears, bananas, grapefruit, or grapes. Serve on a bed of lettuce or other greens.

NUTTY HONEY SWEET POTATOES

6	sweet potatoes	½	cup honey
3	tablespoons margarine	¾	cup orange juice
¼	cup light brown sugar		

Mix the margarine, brown sugar, honey and orange juice and bring to a simmer. Butter a shallow baking dish and arrange in it the pre-cooked sweet potatoes. Potatoes should be peeled and sliced in half. Pour sauce over the sweet potatoes and bake at 300° for 20-30 minutes. Sprinkle with chopped walnuts before serving.

HONEY WHOLE-WHEAT BREAD

If you made the honey butter described earlier, this is just what you need to put underneath it.

½	cup warm water (110°)	¼	cup shortening
2	packages active dry yeast	2¼	cups warm water
½	cup honey	6 to 7	cups unsifted whole-
1	tablespoon salt		wheat flour

Measure warm water in large bowl of electric mixer. Sprinkle yeast over water. Stir to dissolve. Stir in honey, salt, shortening, 2¼ cups warm water and 3½ cups flour. Beat until smooth. Mix in enough remaining flour to make dough easy to handle. Turn dough onto lightly floured board. Knead until smooth and elastic (about 10 minutes). Place in greased bowl; turn greased side up. Cover; let rise in warm place until doubled (about 1 hour). Punch down dough, divide in half. Roll each into rectangle (18 × 9 inches). Roll up, beginning at short side. With side of hand press each end to seal. Fold ends under loaf. Place seam side down in greased 9 × 5 × 3 loaf pans. Cover. Let rise until doubled (about 1 hour). Heat oven to 375° (moderate). Bake 40 to 45 minutes or until loaves sound hollow when tapped. Remove from pans. Brush loaves with soft butter and honey. Cool on wire racks. Makes 2 loaves. (Courtesy of California Honey Advisory Board)

HONEY GINGERBREAD

Here's just the recipe for a gingerbread man for the holidays.

1	egg, well beaten
1	cup dairy sour cream
1	cup honey
2½	cups sifted all-purpose flour
½	teaspoon salt
1	teaspoon baking powder
2	teaspoons ginger
½	teaspoon cinnamon
¼	cup oil

Preheat oven to 350° (moderate). In small bowl, beat egg well. Combine sour cream and honey. Blend into beaten egg. Sift together dry ingredients. Place in large bowl. Add egg mixture to dry ingredients. Beat well. Blend in oil. Pour into well-greased 9 × 9 × 2 pan. Bake 30 to 40 minutes or until done in center. Cool on rack 5 minutes. Remove from pan. Cut in squares. Serve warm. Makes 9 servings. (Courtesy of California Honey Advisory Board)

FRESH ORANGE CAKE

In case you've forgotten how to make a cake from scratch, this one could start you scratchin'.

½	cup butter or margarine
1	cup mild-flavored honey
2	eggs
¼	cup milk
2	tablespoons fresh orange juice
1½	teaspoons grated orange peel
2	cups sifted cake flour
½	teaspoon salt
¾	teaspoon soda

Preheat oven to 350° (moderate). Cream the butter in large bowl of electric mixer. Continue creaming while adding honey in a fine stream. Add eggs, one at a time, beating well after each addition. Combine milk, orange juice and peel. Sift together dry ingredients. Add to creamed mixture alternately with milk mixture beginning and ending with dry ingredients. Beat after each addition. Pour into two greased 8″ round pans. Bake 25 to 30 minutes or until done in center. Cool on wire cake racks 5 minutes. Remove from pans. Complete cooling on racks. Fill and frost as desired.

VARIATION: For Fresh Lemon Cake, use lemon juice and peel. (Courtesy of California Honey Advisory Board)

FROZEN SHERRY WALNUT PIE

This one is so elegant it's bound to impress even your mother-in-law. It's also a good one for you 98-pound weaklings who want to put on some weight.

    9 inch baked pastry shell, chilled
$\frac{1}{3}$ cup sherry
2   eggs, separated
$\frac{1}{2}$ cup mild-flavored honey
$\frac{1}{8}$ teaspoon salt
2   teaspoons vanilla
$1\frac{1}{2}$ cups whipping cream
$\frac{3}{4}$ cup coarsely chopped walnuts
       Additional whipped cream for garnish (optional)
       Walnut halves for garnish (optional)

Place sherry, egg yolks, honey and salt in small saucepan. Mix thoroughly. Cook over low heat, stirring constantly until mixture is slightly thickened. Do not boil. Remove from heat. Add vanilla. Cool mixture in freezer $\frac{1}{2}$ hour, stirring occasionally. Beat egg whites until stiff. Whip cream. Fold egg whites into cream. Gently mix in cold honey custard and walnuts. Spoon into pie shell, mounding slightly. Freeze uncovered. If pie is to be stored, cover tightly with freezer weight aluminum foil. Serve frozen. May be garnished with whipped cream and walnut halves. Makes 8 to 10 servings. (Courtesy of California Honey Advisory Board)

HONEY ICE CREAM

Break out the elbow grease and start cranking! Any kid who wants ice cream has to take a turn at the crank.

1   quart milk
1   quart heavy cream
1¾   cups mild-flavored honey
1   tablespoon vanilla
6   eggs, separated

In saucepan, combine milk, cream and honey. Heat to lukewarm. Stir in vanilla. Chill. Beat egg whites until stiff. Using same beater, beat egg yolks until thick. Carefully blend yolks and whites. Fold into chilled mixture. Pour into chilled freezer container. Add enough milk to fill container to two-thirds capacity. Cover tightly. Set in freezer tub. Follow manufacturer's directions for correct amount of crushed ice and salt. When frozen, remove dasher. Pack down ice cream. Replace cover. Return to freezer tub container. Set in ice and salt until ready to serve. Makes 1 gallon.

HINT: Melt 2 cups chocolate pieces completely in warm milk and cream combined. (Courtesy of California Honey Advisory Board)

MEAD (HONEY WINE)

The use of mead, or honey wine as it is sometimes called, originated in ancient times. It's production in the Middle East is known to predate Christ by at least several thousand years and possibly more. It was a popular drink throughout the Roman Empire and even after grape-base wines began to replace it, mead remained popular in such areas as England and Scandinavia which were not well suited to growing grapes. By the 17th century, sugar from the West Indies became generally available in Europe and this ready availability of sugar caused a general decline in the popularity of honey and beekeeping and hence of mead.

But mead remains today an interesting and versatile drink for the home wine maker. As commonly brewed, mead has an alcohol content of 10 to 14 percent. It can be brewed from nothing more than a mixture of honey and water with a little wine yeast added, or it can be embellished with a number of fruit juices, spices and herbs. It can be light or dark, dry or sweet, still or sparkling.

The amount of honey used per gallon of water can vary from two to six pounds. Two to two and a quarter pounds will yield a sparkling wine. Two and a quarter to three and a half pounds will yield a dry still wine, and for a sweet to rich dessert wine four to six pounds of honey should be used per gallon of water.

The honey-water mixture (which is called "must") should be brought to a slow steady boil for five minutes. This will kill any yeasts in the honey or airbone yeasts that may have gotten into the mixture. After boiling the must for five minutes, remove it from the stove, filter it, and then boil it again for five more minutes. The must is then ready to be poured into an oak cask for fermentation.

You should first pour boiling water into the cask and allow it to stand for five minutes to sterilize the cask and to remove any soluble contaminants. Once this water has been completed poured out, pour in the boiling must. Leave two or three inches empty at the top of the cask to allow adequate room for fermentation. Plug the hole in the cask tightly with a wad of sterile cotton to keep out yeasts and microorganisms. Once the must has cooled to 75-80°F, the wine yeast can be added. The cask should then be resealed with cotton or with a water or fermentation valve.

The cask should then be placed in storage at a constant temperature of 65-70°F. The fermentation will occur in two stages. The first stage, which is the most active, will begin in one or two days and will continue for about one week. The second stage will begin when the first ends and will continue for as much as four months in a rich wine.

Once the second stage of fermentation is complete, the wine may be decanted. To do so, siphon the mead from the first cask into a well-cleaned second cask, but leave about an inch of mead containing any sediment in the first cask. The second cask should then be tightly plugged and allowed to age. Mead can be drunk as soon as six months after it is made, but connoisseurs prefer to let it age six or seven years.

The term "metheglin" is sometimes used interchangeably with mead, although metheglin technically means a mead that has been flavored with such spices and herbs as cloves, ginger, rosemary, or thyme. Other names for mead variations include hydromel, mecomel, pyment, and hippocras. Mulsum, which is not a true mead, consists of wine sweetened with honey. The two recipes given below are suggested as starting points only, since the variations are limitless. Those interested in more detail should contact the Office of Agriculture, Department of Entomology, Cornell University, Ithaca, New York 14850.

English mead is made from the following ingredients:

4	pounds honey	1	gallon water
¼	ounce tartaric acid	1	sliced lemon
	Sulphite	¼	ounce hops
	Wine yeast		

Add the honey and tartaric acid to one gallon of boiling water. Place the sliced lemon in a muslin bag and boil it along with the must for five minutes. Remove the bag toward the end of the five-minute period, skim any scum off the top, and add the hops and sulphite to 100 ppm (two campden tablets). Allow the must to cool to 75-80°F and add the yeast per the directions on the yeast package. From here on, proceed as described above.

And then there's metheglin. Metheglin was invented just to show that making mead needn't be difficult. Start with:

5	pounds honey
1	gallon water
½	cup lemon or orange juice
	Ginger

Bring the water to a boil, add the honey, and allow to boil moderately for five minutes. Turn off heat, skim, and add juice. Filter as necessary to remove all sediment, pour must into a cask and allow it to stand for three to six weeks. Refilter upon removal from cask and add ginger to taste.

HONEY COOKBOOKS

BUTO, HAZEL. *Cooking With Honey*. New York, Crown Publishers, Inc., 1972.

California Honey Advisory Board. *Honey . . . Any Time*. Whittier, California: California Honey Advisory Board, 1979.

ELKTON, JULIETTE. *Honey Cookbook*. New York: Alfred Knopf, Inc., 1955.

KEES, BEVERLY. *Cook With Honey*. Brattleboro, Vermont: The Stephen Greene Press, 1973.

KUSE, JAMES and LEUDKE, RALPH D., eds. *Mamma's Honey Cookbook*. Milwaukee: Ideals Publishing Corporation, 1978.

LIND, SHIRLEY, ed. *Cookin' With Honey*. Rochester, Minnesota: Minnesota Beekeepers Association, 1974.

OPTON, GENE and HUGHES, NANCIE. *Honey Feast*. Apple Pie Press, 1974. (Available from Ten Speed Press, Box 4310, Berkley, CA 94704.)

PERLMAN, DOROTHY. *The Magic of Honey*. New York: Avon Books, 1978.

Index

Index